A Mystical Trilogy ~ 3

Why are we alive?

Our Search for Meaning

~ Book 3 ~

'Awaken to the meaning of life through this three-book series of clear, heartfelt spiritual reflections on spirituality, enlightenment, and the journey within'.

By Ken Luball

Author's Note

'Our Search for Meaning' – Book 3. In this third book of *A Mystical Trilogy* there are 480 short spiritual reflections written in an easily understandable manner, which will readily reflect the spiritual messages about awakening and enlightenment they are intended to share. Each reflection will reveal how you may further your own spiritual journey toward understanding the genuine meaning of life.

My hope writing *'Our Search for Meaning'* was to try to awaken and help others who are awakened more fully understand what enlightenment is so their journey through life may be more fully realized.

As you prepare to begin your search for meaning, do so with an open heart and mind, ready to delve deeper into the mysteries of existence. Let us embark on this spiritual adventure together and, in doing so, discover the answers you are searching for.

Table of Contents

Glossary

Asleep – After we are born we are taught how to survive in the world and what success is. We therefore learn to worry only about our own success and survival in the world, rather than to be concerned about others. This results in living in a self-centered world of prejudice, inequity, and endless struggle. Those who fully believe this are asleep, accepting the status quo as the truth.

Awaken – There may come a time in our life when, despite our success in the world, we begin to question the truth of our self-centered learned beliefs, our ego. When this happens the first quiet messages of the spirit, a piece of god present within every life are sensed, beginning us on an enduring journey to discover meaning in our life.

Ego – The ego is everything we learn, believe, and accept is true after we are born, as we learn how to survive in a self-centered world. Its primary concern is what is best for us; it worries little about others. It also attempts to build up our self-esteem by convincing us of our value in the world.

Enlightenment – The complete acceptance of the spiritual path, allowing the spirit's inherent wisdom and unconditional love to be our primary guide in life. With enlightenment, the ego, our self-centered learned beliefs, assumes a secondary role in our life, no longer influencing the direction of our life choices.

Spirit/ Soul/ God / Higher-Self – An ethereal entity accompanying and inextricably connecting every life to another's. Its purpose is to give our lives meaning by sharing its inherent wisdom and unconditional love to help guide our life's choices.

Spirituality – Spirituality is the belief there is a piece of god, a spirit or soul within every life intimately linking each of us to the other, and, because of this, each life, regardless of our differences, accomplishments, or genus, is important, equal, and connected.

The Meaning of Life

The Meaning of Life

Many form opinions, prejudices about others, observing their appearance, words, beliefs.

The true value of a life though lies not on the outside.

Rather, it may only be found within, where the genuine worth of another has always been.

Do not waste your entire life endlessly searching throughout the world for what is already within your heart.

The answers we seek may not be found in a self-centered world.

They may only be discovered within by embracing the spiritual path, then selflessly sharing our spirit's inherent wisdom and unconditional love to help others discover the spiritual path as well.

When we are born our radiant light shines brightly.

With each passing day though, as we learn, accept, and believe what we are taught about living in a self-centered world, our light begins to dim; for some, their light is barely visible.

When the first quiet messages from our loving spirit within are sensed, we begin on a journey to rediscover our bright light once more.

Once we realize everything we learned was the cause of our darkening radiance, our light will once again begin to shine brightly as it was always meant to do.

Life is an illusion, a play, where we learn our lines so well we believe it to be true.

The truth though, is hidden deep within each of us, behind a superficial façade we learn to project to the world.

We awaken when we first begin to understand this.

We become enlightened when we discard the script, accepting the innate wisdom and loving messages of our spirit in its place.

When we remain in our comfort zone, fearing to challenge our self-centered beliefs, despite our success or accomplishments in the world, we will live a life of mediocrity.

It is only when we confront our fears and challenge the status quo, we may begin to discover our life's true potential.

The ego, our self-centered beliefs, convinces us happiness, success, and meaning may be found in the world.

If we even partially believe this, though we may have awoken, sensing the first messages from our spirit within, enlightenment will elude us.

The spirit, however, asks us to seek our answers only within, where they have always been, and then to selflessly share its wisdom and unconditional love with all others.

It is ironic; we spend our entire life searching for meaning, yet we have always had the answers.

We were simply looking for them in the wrong place.

Within every life is an essence, spirit, soul, god, higher-self.

It matters not what it is called.

It is an ethereal presence intimately connecting each life together, present to give our lives meaning.

When we first sense its messages, then selflessly share its wisdom and unconditional love, the reason we are born, the genuine meaning of our life's journey, becomes clear.

All we must do to awaken is sit in a comfortable chair, close our eyes, quiet our mind, and listen to the silence in between our racing thoughts.

To become enlightened, however, and find the genuine meaning of life, we must then selflessly share our spirit's wisdom and unconditional love to help others understand this as well.

Once we awaken, sensing a deep innate feeling within, we begin to question our life's choices.

Though we may be successful, this feeling will not abate, beginning us on an endless journey of self-discovery.

This awakening may lead to rejecting everything we have learned and believed to be true, as we reevaluate our relationships, job, beliefs.

Instead of only worrying about ourselves, we now wish to help others, so they too may awaken, allowing them to find purpose in their lives as well.

To waste our life living in fear, believing the lies we have been taught about our importance in the world, masks life's true intention.

In the brief time we are alive, to discover our true purpose in life, ignore everything we have been taught about our significance in the world, realizing every life, each with a spirit, a piece of god within, regardless of our differences, accomplishments, or genus, is and has always been, equally important.

We each have two voices we hear within.

One, coming from our mind, is loud, chaotic, often misguided.

The other voice is quieter, arising from our heart.

The latter voice is inherent, accompanying every life, present to guide our lives with its innate wisdom and unconditional love.

When we listen to the softer voice, selflessly sharing its wisdom and love to benefit others, the genuine purpose of our life's journey will become evident.

We truly begin searching for meaning in our life when we start to question the truth of all we were taught and believed to be true.

The path to find meaning is long, often lonely, and very challenging; only a few will reach the end.

It is the journey though, that is the reason we are alive.

By completely accepting the spiritual path through life, then selflessly sharing our spirit's inherent wisdom and unconditional love with all others, the genuine meaning of life will become evident.

I am your spirit, a piece of god accompanying every life to give it meaning.

I am in pain as my infinite wisdom and messages of unconditional love are silenced by the ego, your self-centered beliefs, causing many to needlessly struggle through life.

Listen intently to the silence in-between your chaotic thoughts to hear my messages, then follow its direction to discover the genuine reason for your life's journey.

Most look for inner peace, happiness, and meaning from their job, wealth, family.

Though it may be nice to have all these things, allowing us to briefly experience these feelings, they often disappear with life's next challenge.

To discover genuine inner peace, happiness, and meaning in life, we must first embrace the spiritual path, then selflessly share our spirit's wisdom and unconditional love to improve the lives of all others.

When you look at another, do you see our differences or our similarities?

Most judge others by their differences, observing their race, appearance, sex, and in numerous other ways.

Those, however, who see only our similarities, truly understand the genuine worth of another is not on the outside, but rather may only be found within.

There are but two paths in life: the path of the ego, our self-centered beliefs, or the path of the spirit, equally concerned for all.

Both are important and will accompany each of us throughout our life.

We each, however, may decide which path to predominantly follow.

Most follow the former, accepting and believing all they were taught.

It is only, though, when we allow our loving spirit, the piece of god present within every life to primarily influence our decisions instead, our life will be meaningful as we begin a journey to discover our life's true purpose.

We are alive to reunite with our spirit, our higher-self, accompanying every life, present to give our lives meaning and purpose.

With our birth though and the acceptance of our self-centered beliefs, the ego is formed, often muting the spirit's messages within, making us forget our true purpose in life.

We awake when we first sense our spirit's messages again, questioning our life choices.

We become enlightened when realize our learned beliefs were untrue, and that our true purpose in life is to selflessly share our spirit's inherent wisdom and unconditional love to help others realize this truth as well.

There may come a time in our life, though we have money, material possessions, family, we begin to wonder if there is more to life, a purpose other than what we have achieved.

If we accept this challenge, we will approach a fork in the road.

One path will be straighter; following it will encourage us to enjoy our life by continuing to find meaning in the world.

The other path is much more challenging and curvaceous.

Following this path, our life will change forever as we begin to reevaluate everything we once believed to be true.

Only those choosing the more difficult road may discover eternal happiness, unconditional love, and the genuine purpose of their life's journey.

Humanity may choose to continue to live in a self-centered world of endless conflict, or in a world of infinite love instead.

To understand the former, simply observe the world today and throughout humanity's brief history on our planet.

Senseless death, hunger, homelessness; greed, prejudice, inequity, are but a few of the many challenges resulting from living in such a world.

In a world of love, however, everything would be equally shared.

Every life, regardless of our differences, would be recognized as equally meaningful, important, and deserving to be treated as we ourselves wish to be.

This is the world we are meant to live in.

We just need the courage and wisdom to change our future direction.

Living in a self-centered chaotic world, not wishing to be harmed by others, many embrace fear, prejudice, indifference, choosing to hide their light from the world.

Our light comes from permitting our spirit within to be the primary guide in our life, sharing its wisdom and unconditional love to help others in need.

We each, regardless of our circumstances in life, choose the path we wish to pursue.

Appearance, accomplishments, money, have little to do with our choice.

Only by embracing the spiritual path may our light shine brightly, as it was always meant to do, and may we discover true happiness, inner peace, and find genuine meaning in our life as well.

Though we are all different in many ways, it matters not.
It is our similarities, not our differences, that truly define us.

We each have spark of the divine within, intimately connecting each of us to another.

Only when we all succeed together, uniting our light with the light within others, may our life have genuine meaning and purpose.

Many people search for meaning in their life through religion, money, material possessions, family, and in numerous other ways.

Yet, despite having these things, finding true purpose and meaning in their life eludes them.

Meaning found in a self-centered world is temporary.

To discover genuine meaning, look within, then selflessly share the wisdom and loving messages you sense to benefit all others.

Is there more to life than just to survive and succeed; o make money, have material possessions, a family, and enjoy life's many pleasures?

Those who achieve their goals, while they may have had a successful life, if it was not shared to benefit others, it will have been lived without meaning or purpose.

We awake when we begin to challenge this illusion, sensing the first quiet messages from our spirit within.

We become enlightened when we fully open our hearts, realizing nothing we learned about what success is was true.

Genuine success may only be achieved when we selflessly share our success to help others become successful in their life's journey as well.

After we are born we begin to fall asleep, accepting the self-centered beliefs of the world.

Our sleep deepens as we begin to dream about being successful and enjoying life.

Our repetitive dream turns into an unending nightmare with visions of continual wars, prejudice, inequity, starvation, resulting from our blind acceptance of these beliefs.

We may only begin to wake from our slumber when we start to question if what we learned is true.

We may not fully awaken from our nightmare though, until we realize and accept none of it was.

To find genuine meaning in our life we must challenge everything we were taught and believed to be true.

Though some of what we learn is necessary to survive in the world, everything else often end up dominating our lives, instead of being an aid to our survival as they were meant to be.

We then spend much or all of our life trying to undo the damage done by following this misguided path through life.

Success, material possessions, or anything else found in a self-centered world will not mitigate the harm.

To discover our true purpose in life, listen quietly, then embrace the wisdom and unconditional loving messages you sense, allowing them to now be your primary guide in life instead.

It matters not our race, ethnicity, religion, or any other insignificant differences there may be between us.

Wealth, fame, prestige, have little meaning as well.

We are one people, intimately linked by a universal spirit present within each, alive to selflessly help each other by sharing our inherent wisdom and unconditional love to benefit all.

To truly know another, see beyond their superficial layers and the façade they erect, to the spirit within each.

It is there the genuine value of another may be found.

Differentiating ourselves by race, wealth, beliefs, and in hundreds of other ways, some believe their differences make them superior, their life more important than another's.

This belief is the cause of all of humanities prejudices, inequities, self-inflicted challenges, and harmful actions.

Only by realizing every life, each with a spirit, a piece of god within, despite our distinctions is equally important, may the spiritual evolution of humanity truly begin.

Humanity has a stark choice to make: to continue on the current unsustainable self-centered path it has always followed, or to chart a new path, one that will lead to humanity's advancement and genuine understanding about life's true purpose.

The former will lead to the continuation of the status quo and the eventual end of all life on our planet.

The latter will lead to the spiritual evolution of humanity.

If we do not choose soon, a choice may be made for us.

Imagine a world of abundant love, shared joyously simply in exchange for love returned.

No greed, prejudice, inequity; no learned artificial barriers erected. Ethnicity, race, sex, wealth, would not matter; each would be accepted without judgement.

This is what the world would be like after humanity's spiritual evolution.

We each, by example, may further its beginning by helping others awaken to this reality.

When we merge our conscious mind, physical body, and spiritual soul, we may do astonishing things.

Many would consider the accomplishments miracles, though, just as the great spiritual prophets, we each have this ability within us as well.

By accepting the soul as an equal part of this triad, we may unleash its infinite power.

Doing so, we will discover our life's genuine purpose as well.

Our world is endlessly divided by race, religion, wealth, and in hundreds of other ways.

These divisions only serve to isolate us, justifying our superiority to another.

In truth, there are no divisions.

Every life, though different in appearance, beliefs, accomplishments, is equally valuable.

No one life, each intimately linked by a spirit, a piece of god within, is or ever has been more important or better than another's.

Only when this is finally realized, may the spiritual evolution of our planet truly begin.

Imagine living in a spiritual world, one where everyone selflessly supported and cared about each other in times of need.

Every person would be considered family, not only close relatives, but also, friends, neighbors, and even strangers, selflessly helping each other.

To live in such a world we must discard our self-centered beliefs of family.

Only by unselfishly helping each other, regardless of our many differences, will we all succeed in life and, in doing so, discover life's true meaning as well.

Those who accept and believe what they were taught is true, despite their success in life, if that success was not shared with others, remain asleep, destined to live a life of mediocrity, believing their happiness and meaning will come from a self-centered world; it will not.

True happiness and meaning must first be found within, then it must be selflessly shared to help others find happiness and meaning in their lives as well.

Though we may be surrounded by family, friends, acquaintances, we each believe we must cope with our internal thoughts and demons alone.

We are never truly alone though.

For within every life lies a spirit, a piece of god always present to share its wisdom and love to help mitigate our worries.

To ask for help, listen quietly in-between your random thoughts to the messages you sense within, then follow the loving advice you hear.

Most live their life in a fog, imagining everything they learn is true.

They believe they are experiencing life as it is meant to be, though don't realize they are asleep, having a repetitive dream, never understanding life's true purpose.

They begin to arouse when the first quiet messages of their spirit are sensed, questioning if what they learned was true.

They fully wake up when they accept it all was an illusion, created by the ego, our learned beliefs.

By selflessly sharing their spirit's innate wisdom and unconditional love to benefit others, their fog fully dissipates as the genuine purpose of their life's journey is understood.

Imagine a world where instead of fear dictating our actions, love would, shared selflessly with others sincerely desiring what is best for everyone, rather than only for ourselves.

Everything would be divided equally for the benefit of all.

A world of peace, love, and hope, would replace a world of war, prejudice, and greed.

Though this is not reality, it can be.

For this is what the world would be like after humanity's spiritual evolution.

Accepting the primary guidance of our spirit within, everything in our life will change forever.

Though the ego, our learned beliefs, will continue to help us navigate the everyday trials of life, it no longer will dictate our actions.

Those who truly understand this must then selflessly share their spirit's wisdom and messages of unconditional love, helping all others who seek to discover meaning in their life, find it as well.

Most look for meaning in the world, believing money, material possessions, and enjoying life's many pleasures will allow them to find it; it will not.

Meaning may not be found in a self-centered world.

It must first be discovered within, where the spirit, our higher-self is present accompanying each of us in our journey through life, then its innate wisdom and unconditional love must be selflessly shared to help others find meaning in their lives as well.

The ego is everything we learn, believe, and accept is true; it allows us to survive in a self-centered world, teaching us society's expectations.

Though the ego is an important part of our life, helping us navigate and get by in the world, it is the spirit, the piece of god present within every life, which gives our lives meaning.

On an enlightened level, the purpose of life is to realize this, then primarily follow and selflessly share the loving guidance and wisdom of our spirit within with all others.

Every life, regardless of our differences or genus, has a spirit, a piece of god present within.

Look deeply into the eyes of another to see the soul within each.

Since every life is accompanied by a piece of god, no one life is, or ever has been, better or more important than another's.

Understanding this, selflessly uniting our spirit's love and wisdom with the spirit of others to benefit all, is the reason we are born, the true meaning of life.

It is an illusion that money, prestige, material possessions, or anything else we learned, will bring true meaning or happiness in our life; they will not.

These must first be found within, where our spirit, a piece of god is present accompanying every life.

Only then, by selflessly sharing our spirit's wisdom and unconditional love with others may we find genuine meaning and enduring happiness and discover the reason for which we were born as well.

~ *43* ~

Do not waste a single moment squandering your brief existence chasing illusionary dreams we learned will bring us success, meaning, and happiness.

They will not.

Spend your life instead sharing your essence, the unconditional love and wisdom inherent within every life with all others, making your life truly successful, meaningful, and worthwhile.

Fearful of challenging the status quo, most follow the self-centered path through life.

They, therefore, despite their success in life, lead a life often riddled with doubt, anxiety, and mediocrity.

Our choices in life, however, are not predestined.

We may instead choose to venture off the learned path, detouring inward, merging with our higher-self.

Doing so our life will be full of love, inner peace, and a genuine understanding of our life's true purpose.

I am asleep when I accept the world as it is, believing there is little I may do to bring meaningful change.

I start to wake from my slumber when, sensing a soft voice within, I begin to question my beliefs, wondering if I may help others.

I wake completely when I fully embrace the loving spiritual messages and wisdom from my guide within, realizing there is much I can do to improve the lives of others.

We live in a competitive world, concerned only for our own success and happiness, rather than in a world of cooperation, being equally concerned for what is best for others as well.

From the moment of our birth, we are taught to embrace this false path through life.

We awaken when we begin to wonder if what we learned is true.

We become enlightened when we realize none of it was.

Living in a world of malice and division we judge others by their differences, believing their life is not as valuable as ours.

There may come a time in our life though, a feeling deep within may start to question if this is true.

As we begin to realize it never has been, we now start to see our similarities, rather than just our contrasts instead.

We often spend our entire life chasing a dream we were taught was true.

Believing we will find meaning and happiness if we attain success, wealth, material possessions, most blindly accept the self-centered status quo.

There may come a time in our life though, we begin to question if this dream is real.

It never was.

It was an illusion, propagated by the ego, our learned beliefs, to challenge our choices in life.

We are born enlightened, understanding the importance of every life, regardless of our differences or genus, and the need to selflessly share our innate wisdom and unconditional love, our spirit, with all others.

After our birth though, the ego, our learned beliefs, often becomes the primary director of our life, silencing the wisdom and loving messages of our spirit within.

One day, when we are older, perhaps successful, depressed, unhappy with our life, we may begin to wonder if everything we learned in our life was true.

When we finally realize none of it was, our depression and unhappiness start to fade away, beginning us on a spiritual journey to rediscover what we once knew before we were born and exposed to the beliefs of a self-centered world.

Most remain asleep through their life, believing everything they were taught is true.

Waking up, challenging the status quo, is difficult to do.

Often, when we first begin to arouse, it is our spirit present within, encouraging us to listen to its wisdom and messages of unconditional love.

As its messages become more pronounced, questioning the truth of all we learned, we begin in earnest our journey toward understanding and discovering the true purpose of our life.

The ideas of heaven and hell existing in an otherworldly place originated with religion trying to control their followers.

In reality though, both may be found on earth within each of us.

We are in hell when we blindly accept and follow the false self-centered beliefs of the world.

As we begin to question the truth of these beliefs, we begin our journey toward heaven.

With the complete acceptance of the spiritual path and the realization of life's genuine purpose, to selflessly share our innate knowledge and unconditional love, our spirit within with others, we approach the entrance to heaven's gate.

We begin life knowing only inner peace, infinite happiness, unconditional love, and the genuine purpose for our life's journey: to selflessly share these with others.

As we are taught about life and what is expected of us though, these pure emotions gradually begin to dissipate; many forget they ever existed.

For some there may come a time in their life they begin to sense the soft quiet messages of their spirit within attempting to be noticed.

This begins them on an unending path to remember what they first knew before they were exposed to the false beliefs of a self-centered world.

As we approach enlightenment, accepting the loving spiritual path through life, the disguises others wear begin to fade away.

Instead, we see their genuine spirit within observing the best in others, rather than only their flaws.

An overwhelming desire overtakes us as we now wish to help them realize this as well.

When we are children, we are taught what to believe.

Though some of what we are told is important to help us survive in the world, there are many other things that are not.

Some learn, due to their race, wealth, sex, beliefs, or any of hundreds of other differences, their life is superior, more important than another's.

This leads to prejudice, war, inequity and many other man-made problems and challenges in the world.

The truth is we are all equal, every life meaningful despite our many differences.

No one life, each with a spirit, a piece of god within, is, or ever has been, more important than another's.

Religion divides rather than unites humanity.

These differences have led to prejudice, wars, indifference to the struggles of those who believe differently.

The spiritual messages of the religious prophets, though different in presentation, were identical in their essence: to selflessly share our inherent wisdom and unconditional love, our spirit present within each, with all others, regardless of our differences, for the benefit of all.

It is time to put our self-centered flawed religious beliefs aside.

Instead, we must return to the original intentions the prophets first meant to be shared.

When we talk to another, do we only hear what they are saying, or do we see past their words, to their soul within?

Most hear other's words superficially, influenced by their learned beliefs.

To truly hear another and know their essence, their inherent beauty and love within, listen intently to the genuine meaning beyond their spoken words.

When we become stressed we often depend on our past beliefs and experiences.

We therefore may make rash choices as to what we will say or do.

When this happens, our reactions may greatly harm another.

When the challenges of life become overbearing remain silent, allowing your anxious thoughts to calm, listening closely instead to the quiet loving messages within.

Then, when the moment has passed, choose to react with love, rather than malice.

Many go through life asleep, believing and accepting everything they learned.

As death approaches, when they review their life, the ego, their self-centered beliefs, realizes it will perish when its body does; it therefore releases its hold on their life.

At this time, they begin to realize, though they may have led a successful life, what they once believed important, their job, wealth, material possessions, really was not.

Without the ego's influence, they now may sense their spirit's messages within, telling them only if they selflessly shared their success and love to benefit others, will they have lived a life with genuine purpose and meaning.

Instead of helping others, we harm them.

Instead of loving others, we judge them.

We spend our seminal years when we are children being socialized to accept these self-centered beliefs, then often spend the rest of our life trying to undo the damage and prejudice embracing these views resulted in.

Many have anxiety, stress, worried not only about surviving in a self-centered world, but finding love and happiness as well.

Though money may ease some of their worry, these uneasy feelings do not only arise from our daily struggles.

Looking for enduring love and happiness through being with another person or in the amount of money we make or number of possessions we own will only bring disillusionment, often fluctuating with changing circumstances in our life.

True love and genuine happiness must first be found within, then, to truly experience them, they must be selflessly shared with all others to help them find love and happiness in their life as well.

Many believe only what they see, hear, and can prove, imagining this is all there is to life.

Though they may be intelligent, successful, their lives will never be complete.

To truly realize life in its entirety, a leap of faith is necessary.

Only by also accepting and sharing the unconditional loving messages and wisdom of the spirit, present within every life, will life be fully experienced, and the genuine purpose of our existence be understood.

Most seek happiness, peace, love, and meaning in the world.

Though they may fleetingly find these there, they often disappear with changes in our life.

Only those fully embracing the untethered loving beliefs and wisdom of their spirit within, will discover true happiness, inner peace, unconditional love, and will understand, only by helping others find them in their life as well, will they truly live a life of genuine purpose and meaning.

There are some who harm others with their words, actions, or deeds.

Any injury to another hurts both equally.

Though the person causing the injury may initially feel better, it adversely affects their spiritual journey through life as well.

This debt will then be repaid every day for the rest of their life as their light will dim until they sincerely ask forgiveness for the harm they have caused.

Religion, though well intentioned initially, has divided, rather than united humanity, resulting in prejudice, war, indifference to those who believe differently.

Regardless if we are Buddhist, Muslim, Hindu, Christian, or any other denomination, the one commonality of every belief is to selflessly help everyone, regardless of our differences or beliefs in god, by sharing our unconditional love, the kindness of our spirit, for the benefit of all.

Only when religions embrace their common beliefs, rather than their differences, may humanity truly evolve and the many divisions they have creäted begin to mitigate.

Peace, happiness, and love found in the world are fleeting, temporary, changing with the uncertainty of living in a chaotic self-centered world.

To find genuine peace, enduring happiness, and true love, they must first be discovered within, then, only by selflessly sharing them with all others may they truly be appreciated.

All negative emotions are learned, impeding us from discovering the genuine reason for our life's journey.

Though it is human to have these feelings, they are also the cause of many of humanity's self-inflicted problems, beliefs, and prejudices, affecting the very fabric of our self-centered world.

Only by recognizing the harmful nature of these emotions, embracing instead the unconditional loving beliefs present within each life may genuine change finally be realized.

Every life in the universe is inextricably connected to each other by a common link.

The universal spirit is the underlying power necessary to unite all creation together.

By realizing this, humanity may finally begin to break its egocentric bonds enslaving it in an eternal self-centered fearful existence, freeing them instead to strive to find genuine meaning, love, and purpose in their lives.

Any action shared with unconditional love, harming no one, is courageous.

We are fearless when we stand up, without motive or benefit, to help those in need, doing what is right regardless of personal consequences.

For genuine change to occur, we must be bold, steadfast, daring, always putting the needs of all, before only the needs of ourselves.

Most believe, because of their intelligence, a human life is more valuable than all other forms of life.

Others even believe, because of our differences, the lives of some people are more important than others.

These beliefs are the cause of many of the harmful emotions and problems mankind has inflicted on itself and the world.

Only by recognizing the equal value of every life, regardless of our differences, accomplishments, or genus, may humanity finally begin to understand the true worth of another's life.

We are brought up to accept society's self-centered beliefs about life, learning to be concerned only for our own success and happiness, worrying little about others.

Though we may be successful, these beliefs will lead to a life of mediocrity, devoid of meaning or purpose.

It is only when we realize the equal importance of all others, regardless of our differences, selflessly sharing our excess, success, and unconditional love to help all those in need, the true purpose for our life's journey will become evident.

Money does not ensure we will discover inner peace, find genuine love, and everlasting happiness in our life.

Many who have wealth often struggle every day to find these things.

Yet, there are those who are impoverished who have these in abundance.

Inner peace, love, and happiness may never be found in a self-centered world.

They must first be discovered within, then shared selflessly to help others find them in their life as well.

Living in a spiritual world, anything harming another in any way would no longer be abided.

Prejudice, greed, inequity; hunger, homelessness, war, would end.

This is the world we were meant to live in.

All we lack is the wisdom and sincere desire to make it a reality.

There are those who have tried to bring positive change to the world; using their wealth, voice, actions, they helped many.

Change, however, made in a self-centered world is fleeting, like the wind and rain with the passing of a storm.

Only by first changing ourselves within, then selflessly sharing our wisdom and unconditional love, our spirit, with others, may true change be everlasting.

God exists within every life waiting permission to be released from its self-absorbed bonds.

To break free of these restraints, we must first realize everything we learned since our birth is an illusion; truth only lies within.

With this genuine understanding, we will free the innate wisdom and unlimited loving potential of god within.

Though it may appear humanity does not have a soul as we observe many of the unnecessary struggles and tragedies we inflict on each other and other forms of life, in fact, we have simply forgotten.

Beneath the hatred, prejudice, desire for our own success, is a spirit, soul, god, representing love, acceptance, and hope for the success of every life.

Our soul has simply been waiting permission to be rediscovered.

We are born pure, innocent, knowing only unconditional love.

With our birth though, we learn to protect ourself from the pain of life's injustices.

Many therefore create a façade to shield them from the words and actions of others who wish them harm.

Only by lowering our defenses may we begin to rediscover our life's true purpose: to selflessly embrace and share the wisdom and unconditional loving messages of our spirit within, then help others to remember their true purpose in life as well.

Most limit their view of the world, believing life is restricted by its self-imposed boundaries.

It is only when we challenge our limitations, awakening to the possibility there is more to life than just what we learned, the genuine beauty and potential life offers may be discovered.

Though we are all different in many ways, no one life is, or ever has been better or more important than another's.

Success, if not selflessly shared without motive or benefit, will lead to a life lacking meaning.

Only together, putting all of our superficial differences aside, will we all succeed and discover our life's genuine purpose as well.

Every once in a while, a passing thought may penetrate our protective exterior, our façade, questioning our self-centered beliefs and path through life.

This brief awakening creates a moment of unbelievable calm, inner peace, and feelings of authentic love we wish would continue forever.

With the acceptance of the spiritual path, these emotions will become more frequent, as we begin to selflessly share our innate wisdom and unconditional love, our spirit, to help others experience these extraordinary feelings of calm, inner peace, and love in their life as well.

Humanity believes success in life will be judged by our wealth, fame, job, material possessions, family, or any number of other things we learned would make our lives meaningful.

Though these things may make our lives easier, they do not define who we truly are; nothing in a self-centered world will do so.

Our life will only have meaning when we genuinely embrace our spirit, the piece of god present within every life, then share its wisdom and unconditional loving beliefs to help others awaken, so they too may being to embrace their spirit's messages as well.

Beyond the façade we present to the world is the inherent wisdom and unconditional love of the spirit within.

The pretense we reveal to others is not real.

It is a fiction, created by the ego, our learned beliefs, to bolster our self-esteem.

To truly know another, look past their superficial presentation to their genuine self, their spirit within.

Only then may you know who they truly are.

When we talk with another, our words are influenced by our life experiences.

Therefore, often what we say is superficial, hidden behind a façade created to bolster our self-esteem.

With enlightenment and the understanding of our true purpose in life, the façade no longer is present; all that is left is spirit.

This is the purest form of communication.

When we now converse with another, our spirit's within unite, intimately connecting us as we peer deeply into each other's soul.

Enlightenment is the realization the self-centered path through life we had blindly followed was an illusion.

With the complete acceptance of the spiritual path, understanding there is a spirit, a piece of god present within each life, we realize by selflessly sharing our spirit's wisdom and unconditional love to benefit all others, the meaning of life, the genuine purpose for our existence, will be understood.

~ *84* ~

Life is an illusion, beginning with our birth and the acceptance of all the falsehoods we are taught about living in a self-centered world.

We awaken when we begin to question the truth of what we learned.

The illusion is fully exposed when we realize little of it was true.

When we talk with another, what we hear is often determined by our beliefs and understanding of the world from our life experiences.

To truly hear the message though, listen deeply, beyond the pretense of our life encounters.

Look instead into their heart, hearing their truth unencumbered by our own thoughts.

Many judge others by their appearance, beliefs, accomplishments, and in numerous other ways.

To genuinely know another, however, look beyond their superficial layers, the façade we each project to the world, to their loving essence within.

Only then may we know who they truly are, rather than only the illusion they project to the world.

Gaze intensely into the eyes of another sentient life form.

It matters not if the eyes are human, animal, or another form of life.

If you do, you will see their spirit, a piece of god present within each, intimately connecting us together as one.

Every life, therefore, with a piece of god within, regardless of its accomplishments, appearance, or form, is, and has always been, equally important.

A spirit, a piece of god accompanies every life, present to remind us of our life's true purpose: to selflessly share our excess, wisdom, and unconditional love to help all others, reminding each to do the same.

Instead humanity has chosen to follow the dictates of its self-centered learned beliefs, concerned only for what is best for themselves, rather than others.

Genuine change may only occur when we remember our original purpose.

Anything else, though well intentioned, is transient, ending when greed and indifference once again dictate humanity's future choices.

Look into the eyes of any animal, person, or other form of life.

There you will see a sentient being present, each with a spirit, a piece of god within.

It is not only human beings who have consciousness.

Humanity is not, and has never been, better or more important than any other form of life or each other.

Realizing this furthers our understanding of our life's true purpose.

Though we are each unique, it is our similarities that truly define us.

We are all part of a collective, intimately linked together with a common purpose.

It matters not our differences or genus.

Only together, uniting our spirit's our wisdom and unconditional love present within each, may our lives have meaning.

We are all related, intimately linked together by a shared intent, meant to selflessly support each other.

Every life, regardless of our differences or genus, is equally valuable, having a spirit, soul, god, within helping guide each of us by sharing its wisdom and unconditional love.

By truly understanding this and following the spiritual path through life, our lives will have been lived with genuine purpose and meaning.

The matrix is a world where most are asleep, living in a learned reality accepted as the truth.

To begin to wake from the matrix, listen to the quiet voice you sense within, opening your heart to discover the genuine possibilities life offers.

Listen intently to the quiet messages from your loving spirit within.

Only then may you see beyond the superficial façade of others, to the very soul within another.

No one's life is or ever has been better, more important than another's.

It matters not our wealth, job, race, or any other comparison.

We each, having a spirit, a piece of god within, are intimately linked together, part of a united whole.

Only by combining the unlimited power of our essence within each, may we all succeed and discover the genuine meaning for our life's journey.

Within every life a blinding light exists, present to give our lives meaning and purpose.

Embracing and selflessly sharing this light with others, unconditional love, inner peace, and meaning will enrich our lives.

For those who ignore their light though, accepting the self-centered beliefs of the world, only suffering, struggle, and fear will define their existence.

Most follow the self-centered path through life believing everything they were taught.

The spiritual path, though, is much more difficult, requiring us to challenge the status quo.

Those who follow the former path, seeking true happiness and genuine meaning in the world will not find it there.

To uncover its true location, look within, listen quietly, then fully embrace the wisdom and unconditional loving messages you hear.

When we are first born, our blinding light and radiant love illuminate the entire world.

From that moment though, its brightness begins to dull as we are taught how to survive and succeed in a self-centered world.

We then often spend the rest of our life trying to return to that moment just before our birth, unimpeded by our learned illusions, allowing our light and love to reemerge and shine its light brightly once more.

Many believe happiness, love, and success may be found in a self-centered world; they may not.

Though we may feel these emotions periodically, they are fleeting, often changing with our life circumstances.

Only by first discovering them within, then selflessly sharing them with all others may we awaken, finding not only everlasting happiness, love, and success, but also discovering genuine meaning in our life as well.

Every life, regardless of our differences is linked, connected by a common bond intimately joining us together as one.

Each person, therefore, is part of an extended family, alive to selflessly help each other by sharing their wisdom and unconditional love, their spirit present within each, to benefit all.

The ego, our self-centered beliefs, is necessary to help us survive in the world.

The ego though is meant to assist us, not dominate our life's journey as it does for most.

It is our spirit, however, present within every life, its messages often silenced by our dominant ego, that is meant to give our life meaning.

We are born, the purpose of our life, is to remember our spirit's wisdom and unconditional loving messages, then selflessly share them, without motive or benefit, to help others remember this as well.

A spirit, soul, essence, god is within every life, intimately linking each life to the other.

It matters not what it is called or if that life is human, animal, or any other lifeform.

It represents our higher-self, the unconditional love and wisdom inherent within each life meant to be selflessly shared with all others.

Fully embracing the loving spiritual path through life is the lesson we are alive to understand, the genuine purpose of our life's journey.

Help all in their time of need without expectation of reward.

Even a stranger we may not know, someone who may look different or have disparate beliefs than we have.

This is the world we are meant to live in.

This is enlightenment.

Regardless of any differences between us, we are all human beings, equally deserving to be treated with compassion and aided in our time of need.

Any other belief is a fallacy, perpetrated by the ego, our learned beliefs, to challenge our choices in life.

We are all connected, inextricably linked by a universal spirit, a piece of god, present within each of us.

Only by uniting and sharing our spirit's wisdom and unconditional love, helping each other selflessly, will the true meaning of life be recognized and the lessons we are here to learn be understood.

Those who follow the self-centered path through life, believing they must only be concerned for themselves, when they die, their memory will rapidly fade with the passing of time.

For others though, when their body and ego perish, their spirit will continue to live in the heart of all those whose lives they positively influenced by selflessly helping them in their time of need.

Light or darkness.

Though both remain with us throughout our life's journey, we may choose which path to predominantly follow.

Those who see only darkness accept all they learned, silencing the underlying loving messages of their spirit within.

Though they may be successful, their life will lack meaning.

Those, however, who primarily choose light, selflessly sharing their wisdom and unconditional love, their spirit with others, will instead discover their life's true purpose.

See only the good, disregard the rest.

We all are imperfect, our flaws beginning when we are young as we learn our prejudices, beliefs, and opinions about living in a self-centered world.

Gaze past the façade of another to the inherent kindness within each.

For it is there you will discover the genuine worth of another.

Enlightenment is our destination.

Though most will not reach the journey's end, it is how we live our life that will determine how far we may travel.

By sharing our innate wisdom and unconditional love, our spirit, and selflessly supporting each other despite our many differences, we will travel further on the path toward understanding our genuine life's purpose.

Though certain things we learn are necessary to survive in the world, most are a distraction, mitigating our ability to discover the genuine purpose of our life's journey.

We are born enlightened, aware of our loving spirit within, understanding selflessly sharing its unconditional love and innate wisdom with all others is the true reason we are granted life.

We often forget our purpose in life though, when the dominant ego, our learned beliefs, inhibits our spirit's messages from being noticed.

Then we may spend the rest of our life asleep, trying to remember what we once knew before we were exposed to the false beliefs of a self-centered world.

Some have a sense of entitlement.

Due to their differences or accomplishments, they feel they are superior, their life more valuable than another's.

Though we are all different in our appearance and beliefs, within we are the same, intimately linked together by a universal spirit, a piece of god present within each.

No one life, therefore, each with a piece of god within, is or ever has been more important than another's.

Those who fully embrace their spiritual potential within, release the infinite possibilities life offers.

One need not be a prophet or great religious leader to do this.

Nor do they need to be wealthy, educated, or a certain race or religion.

They only need to sincerely accept the spiritual path, then share their spirit's innate wisdom and unconditional love selflessly to help all in need.

Within every life is a spirit, a piece of god accompanying each to provide meaning in their life.

For most, their spirit's wisdom and messages of unconditional love are silenced by their dominant ego, our learned beliefs.

We awaken when we first sense our spirit's messages.

With our permission, when we allow the spirit rather than the ego to become the primary guide in our life, we will understand the true purpose of our life's journey.

Most are unable to share their authentic-self, their spirit, with others.

They therefore live a superficial life living in fear, seeking happiness, love, and meaning in a self-centered world; they will not find them there.

Genuine happiness, love, and meaning may only be found within, where the wisdom and unconditional love of our spirit lie, then will be discovered when we selflessly share them, without motive or benefit, with all others.

Enlightenment is the complete acceptance of the spiritual path.

Though the ego, our self-centered beliefs, will remain, it will now assume a minor role in our life.

With enlightenment, we selflessly share our spirit's innate wisdom and unconditional love to improve the lives of others.

This will lead to a life of inner peace, infinite love, and to discovering the genuine purpose of our life's journey.

Most are indifferent, apathetic, accepting as normal the many self-inflicted challenges and injustices in the world.

They believe there is little they may do to bring meaningful change; therefore, they surrender to the status quo.

We awaken when we first sense the unconditional loving messages of our spirit within, questioning if we may help others in need.

We begin our journey toward enlightenment when we realize we must try.

Though we are born with a blinding light within, our radiance begins to dull after our birth as we are exposed to the many self-centered beliefs and influences of the world.

To rediscover our light, we must first question if the beliefs we learned and accepted were true may not be.

Only then may we truly begin on a quest to rediscover our brilliant light once more.

Though it is believed humanity has only five senses: hearing, touch, sight, taste, and smell, in truth, there is a sixth sense often ignored. Our sixth sense is our spirit, accompanying each in their journey through life.

Understanding this opens our life to a new dimension of thought, beliefs, and understanding.

Fully embracing its innate wisdom and unconditional loving messages allows us to find genuine meaning in our lives as well.

Humanity's spiritual evolution remains in its infancy.

Religion attempted to further this pursuit, though organized religions eventually adopted man's self-centered interpretation of god, diluting the original messages and meaning of love, compassion, and genuine concern for others.

Only by embracing our loving spiritual nature present within every life, selflessly helping all in need regardless of our many differences, may our evolution become reality and all life and our planet itself, begin to heal from humanity's indifference.

Due to our many differences, some believe one life is more important than another's.

Beginning to question if this may not be true, we awaken.

Understanding it never was, we become enlightened.

The road through life is long, winding, and, at times, quite challenging.

Though there are an infinite number of turns in the road, detouring us in endless directions, the destination is the same: reuniting with our benevolent spirit within.

Though we may be successful, if we do not selflessly share our success and love without motive or benefit, our life will have been led without meaning or purpose.

It is only when we always consider others may our life truly be successful and the lessons we are alive to learn be understood.

Most people look for meaning in their life in the world.

They believe they will find it if they are successful, have material possessions, a family.

Though they may achieve all their goals, true meaning may not be found in a self-centered world.

It must first be discovered within, then selflessly shared with others to help them find meaning in their life as well.

Why are we alive?

The answer to this question, asked for millennia, varies depending on who is answering it.

For some, it is to survive each day by finding food to eat, shelter for safety, warmth for protection from the elements.

For others, it is to make money, buy material possessions, enjoy life's many pleasures.

Nothing we were told though, will answer this question.

In truth, we are alive to embrace our spirit, present within every life, then selflessly share its wisdom and messages of unconditional love to remind others to do so as well.

We are all, regardless of our differences, intimately linked together by a spark of the divine present within every life.

Sharing that spark freely, selflessly, to help others, brings inner peace, infinite love, and genuine meaning to our life, fulfilling the purpose of our life's journey.

Though we may be surrounded by others, many are alone, separated by a wall, a façade, concealing their true self, their spirit, from others.

Their words and interactions are therefore superficial, lacking true purpose or meaning.

Only if they remove their barrier by challenging their self-centered beliefs may they begin to rediscover their spirit within and start on a journey to uncover their true life's purpose: to selflessly share their spirit's wisdom and unconditional love to benefit all others.

Despite our circumstances in life, we each may choose which path through life to follow.

One may lead to success in the world, having wealth, fame, prestige, though this path, if not selflessly shared by aiding others, will lead to a life without meaning.

The other, though not outwardly successful, requires only to selflessly share our wisdom and unconditional love, our spirit, to help others in need.

This path will lead to inner peace, genuine happiness, and discovering our life's true purpose.

Many live in a bubble protecting them from emotional pain and nourishing their self-esteem.

This bubble is our ego, created when we were brought up to believe and accept the world's self-centered beliefs.

Though the ego defends us, it also isolates us from each other and even from ourselves.

The thicker our bubble, the more detached and alone we will be.

It is only when we awaken, sensing the first loving messages from our spirit within, we may begin to end our isolation, now wishing to genuinely help others begin to burst their bubble as well.

Life is an illusion created when we are indoctrinated into society.

We learn what our beliefs, prejudices, judgments are as we are taught how to survive and succeed in a self-centered world.

These ideas form the basis of the person we are to become, often for the remainder our lives.

We awaken when we first begin to challenge these ideas.

We become enlightened when we realize none of them were true; understanding genuine truth and meaning only lie within.

We are each divine, having a spirit, a piece of god within, accompanying every life to enrich our lives with its wisdom and unconditional love.

The messages of our spirit, however, often become hidden behind the dominant ego, our learned beliefs, masking our true life's purpose.

The meaning of life is to return to the transcendent knowledge, present before we were first born, then share our spirit's wisdom and love to help others rediscover their spirit as well.

Every life, regardless of our differences or genus, is part of a universal collective, intimately connected by a unifying spirit present within each.

Apart, continuing to follow the self-centered status quo, we are destined to fail.

Only together, selflessly helping each other, may we all flourish and realize life's true potential.

Regardless of the provocation, there is never cause to hurt another.

It matters not if the slight is physical, emotional, verbal, or in any other manner.

The harm adversely affects us as much as those we inflict it on.

The meaning of life is to share our innate wisdom and love, our spirit, unconditionally with all others.

Anything else, in pursuit of our own gratification only further distances us from our life's genuine purpose.

Within every life is a spirit present to give our lives meaning.

By selflessly sharing its wisdom and messages of unconditional love with all others, our life's purpose will be fulfilled.

The spirit's messages, however, are often muted by the dominant ego, our self-centered beliefs.

It is only when we begin to sense our spirit again that we may start to pursue a new path through life; one that will lead to a true understanding about our life's genuine intentions.

From our first breath we are taught, to live a successful life, we must accept the self-centered status quo.

Only by challenging these beliefs, realizing everything we learned about success was untrue, an illusion designed to have us follow a false path through life, will the genuine reason for our life's journey begin to be understood.

Many search for meaning in their life.

Most seek it in the world believing money, material possessions, family, will allow them to lead a meaningful life.

Though they may achieve their goals, true meaning may not be found in a self-centered world.

It must first be discovered within, then selflessly shared to allow others to find meaning in their lives as well.

Life is an enigma, a paradox.

Most, accepting their learned self-centered beliefs, believe success in life means having a good job, a family, making money, enjoying life.

Though they may have achieved their goals, as they approach death, reviewing their life the paradox of life becomes evident.

They finally understand, life was never about *their* success.

Rather, for their life to have had genuine meaning, their success was meant to be selflessly shared to help all others become successful in their life as well.

Despite our circumstances in life, we each choose whether we will live our life in a world of fear or love.

Wealth, fame, race, ethnicity, will not influence this.

Those who follow the path of the ego, our self-centered beliefs, despite their success in life, will live their life in fear, never truly learning the lessons they are alive to understand.

Only those who challenge the status quo, awakening to the wisdom and loving messages from their spirit within, will begin on a path to discover their life's genuine purpose.

All life in the universe is tethered by a universal spirit, a piece of god present within each, inextricably connecting every life to the other.

It matters not species, form, appearance.

Each life, therefore, regardless of our differences, with a piece of god within, is, and always has been, as important as another's.

After we are born, our beliefs, opinions, and prejudices are formed, often dominating our life's choices.

The underlying wisdom and loving spiritual messages, therefore, present within each life, are often silenced by these self-centered beliefs.

We awaken when the first quiet messages of our spirit are sensed, as we start to challenge all we were taught, beginning us on a journey to discover our life's true purpose.

There are those who have succeeded, become wealthy, famous, enjoyed the best things life has to offer, yet, despite their many accomplishments, their life was only partially lived.

Without also recognizing their spirit within, and selflessly sharing their success with others to help them become successful as well, their life will have been lived without true meaning or purpose.

We are each god, spirit, soul, present within every life.

It matters not appearance, genus, or any other comparison; a small part of the divine lives within everything alive.

Since god exists within all forms of life, no one person or life form is, or ever has been better, more important than another's.

Only together, equally respecting every life, may we find genuine meaning and purpose in our life.

We are all spirit, alive to selflessly share our unconditional love and innate wisdom with all others.

Our differences, beliefs, accomplishments, genus, matter not.

Every life is important; each equally valuable.

Any other idea is an illusion, created by the ego, our learned beliefs, to challenge our true path through life.

Enlightenment is fully accepting the guidance and selflessly sharing the innate wisdom and unconditional loving messages of the spirit, the piece of god present within every life, with all others.

If we even partially still embrace our self-centered beliefs, then though we may have awoken, sensing the first messages from our spirit within, enlightenment will elude us.

After we are born, we are taught what to believe and how to survive in a self-centered world.

For most, the ego, their learned beliefs, dominate their life, mitigating the loving messages of their spirit within.

Only when we awaken, sensing the first quiet messages from our spirit, may we start to end the ego's dominance, allowing us to begin on an endless journey to find genuine meaning in our life.

There are many different beliefs about god.

Whether we call god Allah, Jehovah, Yahweh, or by any other name, it matters not.

Though our beliefs may be different, we are all children of god, equal in every way.

Each believe god is universal wisdom, unconditional love, meant to be selflessly shared, regardless of our religious differences or beliefs, to help all in need.

Many live their life asleep, never realizing everything they learned was an illusion.

There may come a time in their life though, they begin to wake, questioning the truth of what they were taught.

As they confront the many lies they once believed to be real, beginning to understand few of them were true, they start to seek their answers elsewhere.

With the complete acceptance of the spiritual path, they fully wake, realizing, only by selflessly sharing their spirit's innate wisdom and unconditional love to help those in need, will their true purpose in life be understood.

Within every sentient being lies a spirit, a piece of god, intimately connecting each life to the other.

Though each is unique in many ways, every life, each with a piece of god within, regardless of our differences or genus, is, and has always been, equally important.

Only together, respecting the life of each, may we all live a life of genuine meaning and purpose.

When we are children some create a façade, learning to protect themselves from others who are trying to prove their dominance and superiority.

Our façade shields us from pain and discomfort from the harmful words, actions, or deeds of others.

Though this may have happened when we were young, the harm may continue to haunt us as we get older; at times for the rest of our lives.

Only by completely forgiving the injury caused by the other's insecurity, may we awaken, allowing us to move past the pain and to start on a spiritual journey of self-discovery.

We need not have riches or material possessions to live a successful life; a poor, homeless person may do so.

We merely must embrace the wisdom and quiet unconditional loving messages within, then selflessly share them with all others, so they too may live a successful life as well.

Most think power comes from wealth, having an important job, allowing us to have dominance over others.

Though many believe this is true, it is an illusion, created by the ego, our learned beliefs, to distract us from our true source of power and strength.

Real power may never be found in a self-centered world.

Money, prestige, influence over others, will not allow us to find it there.

Genuine power must first be found within, embracing the knowledge and unconditional loving messages of our spirit, then it will only be known when its wisdom and love are selflessly shared with others to help them understand this as well.

Life's Journey

Every life, regardless of our many differences, is and has always been, equally important.

Our body is but a shell housing our spirit within.

Our mind is but an instrument to accept society's self-centered beliefs.

Who we truly are lies not in our achievements or success, but in our essence.

Understanding this is the genuine reason for our life's journey.

There are those in the world who are takers, worried only about themselves, unafraid to take advantage of another.

Others are givers, readily sharing their love and excess with all, sincerely wanting only what is best for everyone.

Though takers may be successful, they will never experience true love, inner peace, genuine happiness, or find meaning in their life.

A giver, however, will find these in abundance, while also discovering life's genuine purpose as well.

Look deeply into the eyes of another; it matters not their appearance, beliefs, genus.

See beyond the outer shell and façade they present to the world.

If we do, we will see a sentient being no different from us, seeking to share its wisdom and universal message of unconditional love.

We are all one, intimately connected, linked by a universal spirit, a piece of god within, and only together, by selflessly helping one another, may we all understand the genuine purpose for our life's journey.

We begin our journey at birth, pure, innocent, without judgment, knowing only unconditional love.

After we are born though, we are exposed to the self-centered beliefs of the world that influence and dominate our lives, often until our demise.

Our thinking, prejudices, and beliefs about the world taint almost all of our decisions.

Instead of the purity and splendor we once knew when we were first born, our life has been altered, distorted by our egoistic beliefs.

By the time we reach the end of our journey, reviewing the life we had led, many will have regrets.

What once began with beauty and love, now is unrecognizable.

We are taught we will find happiness and meaning in our lives by making money, buying material possessions, having a family, enjoying the best things life offers.

Though we may reach our goals, we will never discover true happiness or meaning; these may not be found in a self-centered world.

To find where they truly exist, we must first reunite with our spirit within, then selflessly share its inherent wisdom and unconditional love with others.

Only then, may we not only discover authentic happiness, but also the genuine meaning for our life's journey as well.

Most live in a matrix, asleep, believing everything they learned was true.

Nothing though in the matrix is real.

It is an illusion, fostered by the dominate ego, our self-centered beliefs, to convince us of its reality.

The only truth lies within.

By embracing our spirit's messages and selflessly sharing its wisdom and unconditional love, we may begin to shatter the matrix.

Doing so will reveal life's genuine intentions as well.

Sit silently, look into your eyes in a mirror or reflecting pond.

If you do, you may see a sentient being within returning your gaze, attempting to let you know there is more to life than what we were taught after we were born.

If you peer deeply enough, you will begin to discover the genuine reason for your life's journey.

In doing so, you will also find infinite love, inner peace, and recognize the true meaning of life as well.

Most view life through a tinted lens, seeing an irredeemable world of greed, prejudice, inequity; a world whose harmful emotions and manmade problems are too vast to list.

For some, their lens is so dark, they are almost blind.

Others, though their lens does not totally blind them, they still have difficulty seeing the world clearly, believing success, meaning, and happiness may be found in a self-centered world; they may not.

Sensing the first messages from their loving spirit within, their lens begins to lighten, as they start to question the truth of all they learned.

Their lens further clears when they realize everything they once thought and believed to be true was not.

With the acceptance of the spiritual path, their lens is now clear, as they see the world with unconditional love, wishing to help all others see the world through a clear lens as well.

Before we are exposed to the beliefs of a self-centered world we are enlightened, understanding our genuine purpose in life is to share the inherent wisdom and unconditional love of our spirit, a piece of god present within every life, to selflessly help all others in their time of need.

We then spend the rest of our life trying to return to that moment, before we were first born, to rediscover our life's genuine purpose once more.

Alone, concerned only for our own success, our lives will lack meaning or purpose.

Only together, selflessly helping all succeed, will we discover the genuine reason for our life's journey.

Humanity endlessly divides itself, justifying their superiority to another.

Wealth, race, religion, ethnicity, are but a few of hundreds of ways we differentiate ourselves from each other.

We awaken when we begin to question if these differences are important.

We become enlightened when we realize they never have been.

The reason for our life's journey may not be found in a self-centered world; money, success, fame, will not answer this question.

The genuine purpose of life is to reunite with our spirit, a piece of god within every life, then selflessly share its wisdom and unconditional love with all others, so they too may wish to reunite with their spirit as well.

Look beyond appearance, beliefs, temperament, accomplishments, to see the genuine soul, the essence present within each.

It is there we will recognize our similarities, intimately linked by a universal spirit, a piece of god, uniting us together as one.

Our body is but a shell sheltering our spirit within, present to give our lives meaning by sharing its inherent wisdom and unconditional love to help guide our life's choices.

Those who only see the shell, though they may be successful, will lead a life devoid of meaning or purpose.

Only those who look deeply beyond what they see, to the soul of another, will truly discover their genuine worth.

Many blame others and their life situation for their struggles, never accepting responsibility for their own imperfections.

It is only those who never fault another for their challenges in life, who will truly understand their experiences are simply part of the journey, necessary to discover their life's genuine purpose.

Existence is just an illusion where we all have bit parts in a play about life.

It is only when we challenge the illusion, questioning the truth of all we have been told, may we begin to understand life's genuine possibilities.

The journey through life, seeking purpose and meaning, was always meant to be challenging, searching for answers that may never be found in a self-centered world.

To discover the true meaning of life, look first within, to where your spirit, a piece of god accompanies every life, then selflessly share your spirit's wisdom and unconditional love to help others rediscover their spirit as well.

It is not important when we die; it is how we live that will define our life.

Most believe wealth, prestige, living to old age, allows us to live a successful life.

They do not.

It is only when we selflessly share the wisdom and unconditional loving messages of our spirit within with others that our life will truly be defined when death inevitably approaches.

We each choose how we view life: do we see light or darkness?

When we only see darkness, hate, fear, and distrust will define our life.

Allowing the spirit, however, our light, to guide our path, *regardless* of our challenges in life, love, happiness, and meaning will enrich every day of our life's journey.

There exists within every person an internal battle between the ego, our learned beliefs, and the spirit, our higher-self present within every life.

Though both are important, it is only when we allow the spirit's wisdom and unconditional love to be our primary guide through life, we may awaken and our life's journey to discover genuine meaning and purpose may truly begin.

See beyond the facade others present to the world, to the authentic-self, the essence present within every life.

It is there we will see the genuine beauty of another, as their aura radiates waves of eternal love emanating from their soul.

Everything else we see is an illusion, a myth, dictated by others as truth; it never was.

Before we are born and exposed to life's illusions, we know only the soft soothing loving messages of our spirit within.

It was then, before we were taught to accept the self-centered beliefs of the world, we understood our simple directive was to genuinely care, help, and love each other, selflessly sharing our spirit's wisdom and unconditional love to aid all in need.

This is the reason we are born, the lesson we are here to learn, the genuine meaning of life: to reunite with our spirit within, allowing us to remember our life's true purpose.

Living in a self-centered world, many are like a single drop of rain, fearful only for their own survival.

Despite any achievements, if they are concerned only for their own success, just as a single raindrop is insignificant, their lives will be as well.

If, however, their success is selflessly shared with others, as with many raindrops combining together to sustain life, their life will have been lived with genuine purpose and meaning.

Though it may appear we do not control our own destiny, how we view others and the world is a choice.

Choose to see life's inherent beauty and love, rather than its malice and hate.

In doing so, you will awaken, beginning a spiritual journey of self-discovery.

Many experience anxiety, stress, and other challenges as they strive to survive and find love and happiness in their lives.

Seeking these things in a self-centered world, their struggles will not end, for enduring love and happiness may not be found there.

To rid ourselves of the constant worry, to find genuine love and happiness, quiet your mind, listen to the whispers in between your competing thoughts, then follow the wisdom and unconditional loving advice you are offered.

With every interaction, regardless how fleeting, we share a small part of our spirit with another, changing both your and their life forever.

Even when we die, our spirit will continue to live within them in perpetuity, enriching their journey through life.

Selflessly sharing our spirit's wisdom and unconditional love to benefit others is our true purpose in live.

Do you see the good in others or do you seek out their faults?

We each have a choice how we see and treat others.

See only the good; discard the rest.

Do not judge another.

This is the path through life we were always meant to follow.

Within every life is a spirit, a piece of god present to give our lives meaning.

Our spirit connects each of us to the other, uniting us in a common purpose: to selflessly help each other by sharing its wisdom and unconditional love with those in need.

Only when we do this, ensuring everyone, regardless of our differences, is able to live a life of meaning as well, will our lives have genuine purpose and value.

There is an unrelenting battle within each of us between the ego, our learned beliefs, and the spirit, a piece of god accompanying each life, present to give our lives meaning.

Most follow the former path, believing the self-centered ideas of their upbringing.

Only by following the spiritual path in life though may true change occur and may we discover our life's genuine purpose.

Every life is accompanied by a spirit, a piece of god present within each.

It is here the answers we seek about finding inner peace, eternal love, and genuine meaning in our life may be discovered.

These may not be found in a self-centered world.

Money, material possessions, being with another, will not permit you to find them there.

To truly know inner peace, love, and meaning, they must first be revealed within, then may only be experienced when they are selflessly shared to help others find inner peace, love, and meaning in their life as well.

There are dark periods in our life when we are stressed, trying to survive in a self-centered world.

These opaque shadows begin to lighten when we begin to wonder if perhaps there is a deeper meaning to life.

With the acceptance of the spiritual path as our primary guide through life, our shadow is now barely visible.

Our aura vibrantly shines as we selflessly share our spirit's inherent wisdom and unconditional love with others, so they too may begin to lighten their shadow as well.

~ 180 ~

Believing what we were taught, that happiness and meaning may be found in a self-centered world, though we may be successful, we will never truly know either.

Only by fully embracing our spiritual beliefs, then selflessly sharing our unconditional love and success with others, will we be able to know both true happiness and discover genuine meaning in our life as well.

Many have a façade hiding the real person behind a mask they learned to wear.

Their façade protects them from pain others may inflict on them, though it also imprisons their loving spirit within.

To truly experience life, we must strip away our disguise, allowing us to discover and share our authentic-self to benefit all others.

When we die, the many challenges life had presented us end, as our physical body, the shell housing our spirit, soul, god, within, ceases to exist.

Many die never waking from their lifelong slumber to realize the true purpose of their life's journey was to rediscover their spirit within, then selflessly share its wisdom and unconditional love to help all others understand this as well.

Are we alive just to survive, make money, buy material possessions, live our best life?

Most go through life asleep, accepting this definition as our life's purpose.

There are those though, who awaken during their life, sensing the first quiet messages from their spirit within, beginning them on a quest to discover if there may be more to life than this.

With the complete acceptance of the spiritual path, the reason we are alive, to selflessly share our spirit's wisdom and unconditional love to help others in need, is revealed as the genuine purpose of our life's journey.

Everyone has baggage, incidents and circumstances in their life that affects how they view the world.

Despite the baggage we carry, if we live our life with love rather than fear, shared freely with all others, our image of life will allow us to awaken, beginning us on a journey to discover true happiness, inner peace, and a genuine understanding of our life's purpose.

Most worry only about themselves, wishing to obtain the many benefits life offers.

If their success, however, is not shared with others, then though they may have achieved much and live to an old age, their life will lack purpose or meaning.

If, however, they share their success, selflessly helping others become successful as well, their life will be meaningful, and they will have learned the lessons we are alive to understand.

Regardless of the provocation, there is never a reason to be cruel or unkind to another.

We are alive to love, not hate each other; to show respect, empathy, compassion, and help each other selflessly in our time of need.

Understanding this is the reason for our life's journey.

Happiness found in a self-centered world is an illusion, fostered by the ego, our learned beliefs, to challenge our choices in life.

Though we may believe we are happy, living a successful life, this type of happiness is fleeting, often disappearing with changing circumstances in our life.

True happiness may only be found within, then will only be experienced when it is selflessly shared with others.

With this realization will also come inner peace, infinite love, and an understanding of the true purpose of our life's journey as well.

We are more than just our body and mind.

We are also spirit, a piece of god present within each life to give our lives meaning.

Understanding this, then selflessly sharing our spirit's wisdom and unconditional love with all others will complete our life's quest.

Many believe success means working hard, making money, doing the best things life offers.

They therefore spend their entire life unaware of what is truly important.

When death approaches, our spirit, previously silenced by the dominance of the ego, our learned beliefs, may now clearly be heard.

It is then we finally understand nothing we once believed to be important truly was.

We now realize the true reason for our life's journey was to selflessly help each other by sharing the wisdom and unconditional love of our spirit to help ease the burdens others may have to endure.

When we are young we learn to protect ourselves from pain caused by others seeking to harm us with their words, deeds, or actions.

We therefore erect a barrier around our heart, encasing our spirit within, preventing our authentic-self, our spirit, from revealing itself.

It takes courage to expose our heart, though unless we do, we will always be living a superficial life, fearful, worried about being hurt again.

To live a meaningful life, to learn the lessons we are alive to understand, we must risk pain by freeing our spirit, then sharing its wisdom and unconditional love to help others realize they too must try to expose their heart as well.

The spirit, a piece of god present within every life, gives our lives meaning.

By selflessly sharing its innate wisdom and unconditional love to benefit others, we will have understood the genuine purpose of our life's journey.

Ignoring its importance and effect on our lives though, is the cause of much stress, anxiety, and other problems many experience throughout their life.

Only by uniting our mind, body, and spirit, may our journey through life be truly successful and our anxiety and stress mitigated.

Believe the quiet subtle messages within.

They emanate from the spirit, god, soul, present within every life.

By following the loving guidance and wisdom they provide, they will lead to inner peace, true happiness, unconditional love, and a genuine understanding of our life's purpose.

As we realize death is imminent, many will review their life.

At this time, most begin to question if what they once believed to be important, truly was.

They now realize the money, material possessions they once believed necessary, never were, recognizing nothing they acquired or accomplished during their life will accompany them after they die.

They finally understand only those whose lives they sincerely influenced, by selflessly sharing their excess and unconditional love with, will be the only ones to truly define their life's legacy.

Every life has an inherent memory, present within each of its cells, in its DNA, when they are first born.

This memory is found in every lifeform throughout the universe, emanating from its spirit, a piece of god within.

Remembering and selflessly sharing the spirit's innate wisdom and unconditional love to aid others, gives our life meaning and is the real reason we are each born.

God, spirit, soul, higher-self, it matters not what it is called, is an ethereal entity present within every life, accompanying and intimately linking each life to another's.

It represents universal knowledge and unconditional love meant to be selflessly shared with all others.

To understand the genuine meaning of life, sit quietly, listen to the silence in between your wandering thoughts, then fully embrace your spirit's wisdom and love as your new direction through life.

When we live our life with fear, worried only about our own survival and success, each day we fear both life and death.

If, however, we live our life with unconditional love instead, we fear neither, freeing us to fully embrace life, making each day significant and meaningful.

With our birth our education begins, as we learn to accept the self-centered beliefs of the world.

Doing so, our light, our spirit within, begins to dim, teaching us to pursue happiness, meaning, and success in the world; they may not be found there.

To find true happiness, meaning, and success, we must first rediscover our light within, then share it selflessly to help others rediscover their light as well.

Every life has a spirit, a piece of god present within each, intimately connecting each life to another's.

Our spirit's purpose is to give our lives meaning by sharing its inherent wisdom and unconditional love to help guide our life's choices.

With our birth, however, it soon assumes a secondary role in our life, often forgotten, obscured behind our self-centered beliefs.

We awaken when we first begin to sense our spirit within.

We become enlightened when we allow our spirit to become the primary guide in our life, as it was always meant to be.

We are all on the same journey through life.

Regardless of our circumstances, accomplishments, or differences, no one life is, or ever has been, more valuable than another's, each having a piece of god, a spirit within.

Only by recognizing this and selflessly helping each other in our time of need, will we all succeed and live a life of genuine meaning and purpose.

When we die, only our body and ego, our learned beliefs, perish.

Our spirit, however, present within every life, is eternal, returning to a higher vibrational plane until it once again unites with a new life.

Our spirit though, also continues to exist within the spirit of all those it had selflessly helped in their time of need.

Those who live their life concerned only for themselves, though they may have accomplished much, will have led a life without meaning or purpose; their spirit will soon be forgotten.

Those, however, who sincerely helped others, without motive or benefit, their spirit will forever continue to influence the lives of all they helped during their life as well.

By sharing our spirit's wisdom and unconditional love with others, we may each change the world.

When we fully adopt the spiritual path through life, our extraordinary inherent abilities to aid others in need is unleashed.

Selflessly sharing our radiant light, our spirit with others, is the genuine reason we are born, the meaning of our life's journey.

As life races by, we each anxiously search for happiness, meaning, and love in the world.

Though we may find them temporarily, they often fade due to stress, chaos, or changes in our life situation.

To find enduring happiness, meaning, and love we need only look within, where the answers we have sought have always been, then selflessly share them with others, so they may experience these extraordinary feelings in their life as well.

Spirituality is the belief there is a spark of the divine within every life, intimately connecting each life to the other.

It matters not our differences, accomplishments, or genus.

Every life, each with a piece of god within, is equally valuable.

Uniting our spark of the divine with another's amplifies god's energy exponentially and is the genuine reason for our life's journey.

We learn money, fame, prestige, define a successful life; they do not.

Success, as defined by a self-centered world, is an illusion, a mirage.

A poor, unknown homeless person may lead a far more successful life then someone who is wealthy or famous.

True success may only come from understanding our genuine purpose in life: to fully embrace our spirit, a piece of god present within every life, then selflessly share its wisdom and unconditional love to help others awaken so they may remember their true purpose in life as well.

Regardless of our circumstances in life, we each choose our own destiny.

If we blindly follow the self-centered beliefs of the world, we will live our life in fear, never truly understanding the reason we were granted life.

If, however, we choose to live our life with unconditional love instead, inner peace and genuine meaning will enrich our life, fulfilling our true destiny.

No one, regardless of their circumstances in life, may go through life unscathed.

Every experience, both good and challenging, is a lesson.

To discover the genuine purpose for the encounter, look within, where the answers about the importance of these lessons have always been.

We all, each with a spirit, a piece of god within, regardless of our appearance, beliefs, or genus, are part of an infinite universe, intimately connecting each of us to the other.

Only united, realizing the equal importance of every life, may we all flourish; apart, we are destined to fail.

We all experience pain in life.

It matters not if the injury is verbal, emotional, or physical.

For some, the pain is intense, due to loss or accident.

We each, though, choose how we will react to our pain.

Do not internalize the pain, blaming others; this will only lead to a life of regret, misery, and anger.

Instead, learn from it, sincerely forgive those who are the cause, using the pain to further discover the lessons we are alive to understand.

Within each person is both darkness and light.

Most live on a spectrum between the two.

Those who see only darkness, despite their success in the world, are destined to live a life of conflict, struggle, and loneliness.

We may choose, however, regardless our circumstances in life, to live our life with light instead, as we were always meant to do.

When we do this, we will always see the best within others, rather than only their flaws.

Though we may be successful in life, despite having money, material possessions and enjoying life's many pleasures, some may feel an emptiness within.

This feeling arises from our spirit, present within every life to give our lives meaning by sharing its inherent wisdom and unconditional love to help guide our life's choices.

It is trying to let us know our definition of success is flawed.

As we begin to reevaluate our life, we start to realize our life will only truly be successful when we selflessly help others succeed in their life as well.

There are some, though successful, who may begin to wonder if their success truly defines their life.

Often, this happens around mid-life, though may occur anytime, as the first quiet messages from their spirit within are sensed.

They begin to reevaluate their job, relationships, beliefs, and everything else they once believed to be true.

Money, prestige, fame, no longer dominate their view of the world.

They begin to understand, selflessly helping others find success in the world as well, is the genuine reason we are born, the purpose of our life's journey.

We are both body and essence.

Our body is mortal, perishing along with our ego upon our death.

Our essence, however, is eternal, joining each life in the beginning, returning to a higher vibrational level when its body dies.

Though they are separate, our chi is the bridge connecting them together.

Both will influence us throughout our life.

It is only when our essence, rather than ego becomes the primary guide in our life, the energy of our chi begins to radiate inner peace and unconditional love, allowing us to start on a journey to understand the genuine purpose of our life.

We are born enlightened, with the inherent wisdom and knowledge of the universe within our very being.

With our socialization though, our self-centered views, beliefs, prejudices, and opinions of the world are formed.

The irony of life is we then often spend the rest of our life trying to return to what we once knew to be true before we were first born.

We each face darkness and light throughout our life.

Darkness does not arise from within; it comes from the self-centered world around us and is internalized.

Within there is only light, unconditional love.

Darkness, learned after we are born, is the cause of many of humanity's self-inflicted problems and harmful emotions.

It need not control our choices though.

We may instead chose to allow light to be our primary guide, furthering our understanding about the genuine purpose of our life's journey.

Our lives are easiest when we go along with the status quo, accepting the many challenges living in a self-centered world result in.

It is only when we decide to confront the norms society dictates, questioning the truth of what we were taught, that we begin to reevaluate our life's choices, starting us on a thought-provoking path to discover the genuine purpose of our life's journey.

After we are born, the lie begins.

Perpetrated by the ego, our learned beliefs, we learn to survive and be successful in a self-centered world, we must be concerned only for ourselves, rather than to worry about others.

Most people live their entire life never recognizing this fiction was untrue.

It is only when we start to question the lie that we may begin to confront the deception, beginning us on a journey to discover our life's true purpose.

The irony of life is we are born enlightened, forget, then spend the rest of our life trying to return to that peaceful loving state we once knew before we were first exposed to the chaos of living in a self-centered world.

Accepting what we learn is true is the cause of our forgetfulness.

We reawaken to our essence's presence when the first quiet messages from our spirit within are sensed.

With the complete acceptance of the spiritual path, accepting its innate wisdom and loving guidance as our primary guide in life, we may finally once again return to our natural state.

Within each of us lies an infinite force able to transform the world.

Though it is often hidden behind the self-centered illusions we were taught to believe, it awaits our permission to be heard.

To do so may cause great distress, as we must confront the many falsehoods we once believed to be true.

Only when we do this though, may we not only discover meaning in our own lives, but help transform the world as well.

Sense the beauty and aroma of nature and all who inhabit it.

See the radiance vibrate from its core, as each life linked together comes alive in their interactions.

The loss of even one life, no matter how insignificant, affects all.

Only together, respecting the right of each to exist, may our world evolve, allowing each to attain their full potential.

Many believe there is little they may do to improve the lives of those who are struggling.

This belief, fostered by the self-centered ego, our learned views of the world, encourages the endless hardships so many endure.

After we awaken, sensing the first loving messages from our spirit within, we begin to wonder if change is possible.

As the messages become clearer, we dedicate the rest of our life to making this change a reality.

Our purpose in life is to return to the peaceful harmony, eternal love, and infinite knowledge we once possessed before we were born, when we knew only our spirt within.

It was not until we were exposed to the false beliefs and chaos of a self-centered world, that we forgot our genuine purpose in life, creating the many challenges we would encounter in our life's journey.

Some fault others, their life circumstances, or a myriad of other things for their misfortunes and struggles in life.

Only those who embrace every life challenge with strength and courage, never blaming another, will face the affront and understand the lessons being offered.

Beyond the facade we learn to project to the world when we are young, lies the purity, wisdom, and unconditional love of our spirit, present within each.

In many it is hidden by their dominant ego, our self-centered learned beliefs about life.

Our spirit is simply awaiting our consent to share its wisdom and unconditional loving messages with us, beginning us on a journey to rediscover our true purpose in life.

When a wrong is committed, we must no longer remain silent.

It matters not if the injury is physical, verbal, ignoring the needless struggles of others, or in any other manner.

Anything harming another in any way is always wrong; there is never a time when it is not.

If we see anything we would not wish happen to us, that is the measure to be silent no more.

As we age, entering the twilight of life, many begin to wonder if their life was worthwhile, meaningful.

Though they may have led a successful life, if they did not selflessly share their success to help those less fortunate, their life will have been lived without purpose.

Only by sharing our unconditional love and excess freely to help all in need, without motive or benefit, will our life have been truly worthwhile and meaningful.

An enlightened world would not allow anyone to face life's challenges alone.

Rather, they would help the discarded, the untouchables, the poor, all those who are often overlooked in their time of need, providing refuge to the homeless, food to the hungry, rest for the weary.

Every life, regardless of their differences or circumstances in life, must be lovingly embraced, allowing each to live a life of dignity and meaning.

The ego, our self-centered beliefs, is formed with our birth as we are taught how to act, think, and treat others.

Since we are children, we believe everything we learn, hear, and observe.

Some therefore believe they are special, better than others, due to their skin color, religion, sex, or any of hundreds of other differences between us.

It is only when we awaken, sensing the first messages from our loving spirit within, that we may begin to question and challenge these beliefs, beginning us on a journey of to discover our true purpose in life.

There may come a time in our life we come to an inflection point, deciding if our life has been meaningful.

Though we may have achieved our goals, there is an uncertainty if there may be more to life.

As we begin realize there is, we start to challenge our self-centered beliefs, forever changing the direction of our life's journey.

Life was so simple when we were young.

We learned to be nice to others, care about those who were different from us, share our toys so everyone could enjoy them.

As we got older though, our beliefs began to change as we accepted society's self-centered views of the world.

We awaken when we begin to remember our childhood beliefs, hearing the first messages from our spirit within.

As the messages become more prominent, we begin a journey to return to the pure, genuine, caring values we first learned when we were young.

Most go through life asleep, doing everything they believe they are supposed to do.

There may come a time in their life though, sensing the first quiet messages from their spirit within, they begin to reexamine their life, wondering if there may be more to life than just what they were taught.

When this happens, their life will change forever as they embark on a new path, one that will lead to understanding the genuine purpose of their life's journey.

The endless noise within each of us and in the self-centered world inhibits the quiet messages of our spirit within from being heard.

Though our spirit frequently attempts to share its wisdom and messages of unconditional love, it often appears as an echo, its voice muffled in the distance, preventing us from hearing it clearly.

We awaken when we first sense its soft cries, allowing the chaos and clatter within us begin to dampen.

With the complete acceptance of the spiritual path, the noise within becomes silent, as the echoes in our life disappear.

As death approaches, we often reflect on our life choices.

We wonder, though our life may have been successful, if the choices we made allowed us to find true happiness, peace, love, and meaning in our life.

It is then, when the ego, our learned beliefs, releases its hold on our life, we finally realize, though we may have believed we found happiness, peace, love, and meaning, in truth we never did.

We now understand these things may never be found in a self-centered world.

To truly experience what they are, they must first be discovered within, then selflessly shared, without motive or benefit, to help others find happiness, peace, love, and meaning in their life as well.

Many view success as wealth, fame, having a prestigious job, enjoying life's many pleasures.

In truth, success may not be found in a self-centered world.

It must first begin by freeing our spirit within, then selflessly sharing our success with all others, so they too may become successful in their life as well.

Times of struggle offer a unique opportunity to reassess our lives.

Those who find blame in others for their struggle, will go through their life without understanding the reasons these challenges presented themselves.

If, however, we embrace the struggle, learn from each encounter, it may lead to a time of great change, as we begin to reevaluate our life choices.

In life, there is but one final destination: reunification with our spirit, present within every life.

To reach our goal, however, there are many detours challenging us throughout our life.

The more we accept our self-centered beliefs, the more difficult our journey will be.

When we awaken, sensing a loving presence within, our detours begin to lessen.

Though few will reach their ultimate destination, it is the journey getting there that is life's true purpose.

When we judge another by their differences, we remain asleep.

When we begin to wonder if these may not be important, we awaken.

It is only when we realize, though we are all different, every life is equally important, intimately linked by a spirit, a piece of god within, that we may truly begin our journey toward enlightenment.

Most of us try to balance our desires and needs, with our hope to discover meaning in our life.

There are times though, due to stress, anxiety, loss, we may lose our balance, trying just to survive the day.

It is then we must realize we are not, and never have been, alone in our struggle.

There to help us in our time of need is our spirit, a piece of god present within every life.

To regain your balance, quiet your mind, listen to the silence in between your chaotic thoughts, then follow the wisdom and embrace the unconditional loving messages you sense within.

We each control our own destiny.

For those influenced by their learned beliefs, their fate is often predetermined, as they strive to succeed in a self-centered world.

Though they may achieve their goals, their life will be devoid of meaning or understanding; their destiny unaffected.

Those, however, who awaken, sensing the first messages from their loving spirit within, may alter their destiny, as they seek to discover the genuine purpose for their life's journey.

When we are first born, the purity of our life is unobstructed; no impediments obscure our vision.

With our birth, however, our self-centered beliefs and opinions about the world is formed, clouding what we see.

For some, believing everything they were taught, they are almost blind.

Only when we awaken, sensing the first quiet messages from our spirit within, may our sight once again begin to clear, as we seek to rediscover the genuine purpose of our life's journey.

Regardless of race, ethnicity, wealth, or any other comparisons we learned may make, one life is not more important than another's; every life is equally valuable.

Only by selflessly helping each other, sharing our excess and unconditional love with all in need, may our life be meaningful and the genuine purpose of our life's journey be understood.

Living in a self-centered world, many harden their heart, not allowing the pain and struggles others endure to penetrate their outer shell.

Though this allows them to ignore the suffering of others, it also inhibits their ability to truly understand their life's purpose.

To do so, they must expose their vulnerable heart, risk pain, and selflessly help others in their time of need.

Only then, may their life's true purpose be realized.

As I approach the twilight of life, I wonder where all the years have gone.

I never knew genuine love, inner peace, or true happiness, though I thought I did.

I now realize these pure heartfelt emotions could never be found in a self-centered world.

Rather, they have always been a part of me.

All I had to do to experience them was open my heart, then selflessly share its unconditional love with all others.

Many look for love, happiness, inner peace, and meaning in their job, wealth, or family.

Though these may briefly convey these feelings, anything achieved in a self-centered world is fleeting, often disappearing with our next challenges in life.

Genuine enduring love, happiness, inner peace, and meaning may only be found within, then they must be selflessly shared to help others discover them in their life as well.

Most look for happiness by making enough money so they may enjoy life's many pleasures.

With the acceptance of the spiritual path though, we realize what we once believed brought us happiness, never really did.

True happiness found in a self-centered world is an illusion, fleeting, often passing with changing circumstances in our life.

It may only be found within by selflessly sharing our spirit's wisdom and unconditional love to help others find true happiness in their life as well.

Unpleasant experiences from our past may bring back stressful memories we first felt when the event happened, triggered by a similar experience happening now.

Only by sincerely forgiving those who instigated the memory, allowing us to let go of our past, may we live a more complete meaningful loving life.

When you listen to another, stop talking, do not formulate an answer, quiet your mind, pay attention intently.

If you do, you may hear the underlying wisdom and messages of unconditional love residing within every life.

Though it may be difficult to hear, it is there, hidden deeply behind the façade we learn to project to the world.

It is only then you will truly know the meaning of the other's words.

A conflict rages within every person between the spirit, present to give our lives meaning, and the ego, our self-centered learned beliefs.

To discover your true purpose in life, allow the spirit to be your primary guide, then selflessly share its wisdom and unconditional love with others to remind them to do the same as well.

Every person, regardless of their circumstances, may lead an extraordinary life.

Wealth, material possessions, fame, prestige, or any other accomplishments in the world will not determine this.

An extraordinary life may only be lived by discovering the genuine reason for our life's journey: to reunite with our spirit within, then selflessly share our excess and spirit's wisdom and unconditional love to benefit all others.

Our actions may help others, though they may also cause great pain.

Regardless of the provocation, there is never a reason to harm another.

It matters not if the injury is verbal, physical, or in any other manner.

Every life, each with a soul, a spirit within, is as valuable as our own.

Only when we truly understand this may we awaken, beginning us on a path to discover our true purpose in life.

We live in a self-centered world where success is synonymous with winning.

We believe we will win, proving our superiority to others, if we are wealthy, powerful, own more possessions, or any of hundreds of other ways humanity defines success.

In truth, despite our success in life, winning may never be achieved alone.

It may only be accomplished when we all win together, selflessly helping each other become successful in life as well.

Within every person, two competing entities battle to dominate our life: the ego, our learned self-centered beliefs, and the spirit, present to give our lives meaning by sharing its inherent wisdom and unconditional love to help guide our life's choices.

Though both are important and will influence our lives, it is the one we predominately follow that will determine if our life has been meaningful.

With our permission to allow the spirit, rather than ego to be our primary guide in life, we begin on a path to understand the genuine purpose of our life's journey.

Most believe they must confront their challenges in life alone.

When we awaken, sensing the first loving messages of our spirit within, we begin to understand we have never been alone.

To help us endure our trials in life, we only need to ask our spirit to share its wisdom and unconditional love to help guide our life choices.

After we are born, we learn to play the game of life.

We develop certain beliefs, prejudices, views of a self-centered world, as we learn to be concerned only for ourself, rather than to worry about others.

We believe we win the game when we succeed in life by making money, allowing us to enjoy life's many pleasures.

Though many think they have won this game, they have not.

We may only win the game of life when we accept the guidance of our spirit, a piece of god present within each life, then selflessly share its wisdom and unconditional love with others, so they too may win the game of life as well.

Some may erect barriers, a façade, to protect them from pain others wish to cause them from their words, actions, or deeds.

Though their shield aids them in this endeavor, it also distances them, not only from others, but from their genuine self as well.

To rediscover who we truly are, we must purge our protective shell, setting our spirit free to guide our life with its wisdom and unconditional love.

Only then may we awaken and truly begin to understand the genuine possibilities life offers.

Ask not what the world can do for you; rather, ask what you can do for the world.

This is the spiritual path through life, understanding the equal importance and synergy of every life.

Those who accept this challenge, selflessly helping others who are struggling, will discover enduring love, true happiness, and the genuine purpose of their life's journey.

Humanity's definition of normal has become distorted.

They believe war, random violence, prejudice, homelessness, hunger, are a normal part of life; they are not.

They are the result of living in a self-centered world, concerned only for ourselves, rather than others.

In a spiritual world, normal is being equally concerned for every life, regardless of our differences, and sharing our unconditional love and excess equally with all in need.

This is the path we were always meant to pursue, the lesson we are here to learn, the true purpose of our life's journey.

The meaning of life is to follow the spiritual path, understanding we are meant to help not harm, love not hate others.

Our path, though, has many twists and turns.

This is the result of the ego, our self-centered beliefs, which distracts us, detouring us in the wrong direction.

Our purpose in life is to remember our original destination, reuniting with our loving spirit within, then selflessly helping others do the same as well.

It is how we live our life that will determine our destiny.

If we live it primarily for ourselves, then though we may become successful, live to an old age, our destiny is to live a life of mediocrity, lacking meaning or purpose.

If, however, we begin to sense the wisdom and loving messages of our spirit within, we start on a path to control our own destiny, as we seek to discover our life's genuine purpose.

The numerous struggles, both in the world and within each of us, may torment our lives every day.

Our internal battles, often caused by the acceptance of our self-centered beliefs, may result in depression, stress, and anxiety.

By challenging these beliefs, we may begin to heal.

By selflessly helping others in need, we may further mitigate our symptoms and begin on a path to discover genuine meaning in our lives as well.

It matters not if we know another, they are strangers, or if they appear or believe differently than us.

We are alive, our purpose in life is, regardless of our differences, to selflessly share our wisdom and unconditional love, our spirit, with others to benefit all.

To rediscover our bright light, our spirit, we must journey within to our very core.

It is there, hidden from view by the acceptance and dominance of the ego, our self-centered beliefs, that our spirit, the piece of god present within every life, waits our permission to share its wisdom and unconditional loving messages.

When we finally allow our spirit to be heard, we begin on an enduring journey to understand the genuine reason for which we were born.

Before we are born, we are serene, at peace, knowing only unconditional love.

It is not until we enter the world and socialized to accept the self-centered beliefs of humanity, our understanding about life's true purpose becomes distorted.

The irony of life is we then spend the rest of our lives trying to return to the calm, peaceful loving thoughts we once knew before we were first born.

Though we are all different in many ways, no one person's life, regardless of wealth, beliefs, race, or any other possible comparison, is better or more important than another's.

We are one people, intimately linked by a loving spirit, a piece of god within, connecting each of us to the other.

Understanding and accepting this is the genuine purpose of our life's journey.

We each choose how we will view life.

If we only see darkness, the worse in others, we will spend our life living in fear, never understanding our life's true purpose.

If, however, we see light, we will instead see the best in others, helping them to rediscover their light, present within each, as well.

We are alive to share our spirit's wisdom and unconditional love, present within each life, selflessly to benefit all.

Anything else found in the world, believed to bring meaning to our life, is an illusion, fostered by the ego, our self-centered beliefs, to challenge our life's true purpose.

Harming another, whether verbal, physical, emotional, or in any other way, adds to our spiritual debt, making it more difficult to truly understand the reason for our life's journey.

Only by selflessly helping others, without motive or benefit, may this balance be lessened, and the genuine purpose of our life's journey be understood.

To truly help another, see beyond their façade, recognizing their hidden essence, their spirit, present within each.

Doing so, will not only allow you to aid someone, but may also awaken them to the genuine possibilities life truly offers.

When we die, only our body and ego, our learned beliefs, perish.

Our spirit, however, present within each, returns to a higher vibrational plane to join others awaiting their next life's journey.

Our spirit though, also remains with all those we selflessly shared our wisdom and unconditional love with during our life, becoming part of their spirit to be shared with others as well.

Most worry only about themselves and their success in the world, constantly working, striving to enjoy life, rather than spending more time selflessly helping others and with those they love.

It is not until they approach death though, that they may begin to realize, if they had only understood this earlier in their lives, their life would have remembered and worthwhile, rather than forgotten and lived without meaning or purpose.

Those who accept the self-centered views of the world, though they may be successful in life, live to an old age, will never understand life's true purpose.

Others though, who begin to question what they were taught, may never return to their illusionary life.

Instead, they will search endlessly for meaning and to discover the true purpose for their life's journey.

The ego is everything we learn and believe to be true after we are born.

Its directive is self-serving, always taking care of itself, rather than being concerned for others.

Our spirit, however, is inherent, present within every life, existing to provide guidance, wisdom, and meaning in our life.

For most, the spirit's messages are silenced by their dominant ego.

For some though, they may awaken during their life, sensing the first quiet messages from their loving spirit within.

When this happens, they begin to question the truth of what they were taught.

As they begin to realize everything they learned was untrue, the spirit replaces the ego as their primary guide in life, allowing them to now seek the true meaning and purpose for their life's journey.

We are born with a blinding light, shining so brightly darkness cannot penetrate it.

Our light, representing universal wisdom and unconditional love, radiates from our spirit, a piece of god present within every life, there to give our lives meaning and purpose.

With our first breath though, our light begins to dim, as we learn about the self-centered world we will live in.

The more we accept these beliefs, the dimmer our light becomes.

To begin to rediscover our light once more, we must realize most of what we were taught was untrue, then embrace the loving spiritual path we were always meant to follow instead.

Many believe the reason we are born is to get a good job, make money, buy nice possessions, have a family, enjoy the best things life has to offer.

Nothing listed above though is the true reason we are alive.

We are born to reunite with our spirit, a piece of god within, then selflessly share its wisdom and unconditional love with all others, so they too will remember their purpose in life as well.

With this realization, we will have learned the lesson we were born to understand.

Our aura darkens as stress and daily challenges of living in a self-centered world radiate from our very being.

To unburden our lives, lighten our aura, begin to discover the genuine meaning of our life's journey, sit quietly, listen silently to the subtle messages in-between your racing thoughts, then trust its wisdom and loving guidance to change the course of your life forever.

The ego, our self-centered beliefs, considers only what is best for itself and us.

The spirit, however, a piece of god present within every life, not only considers this, but also what is best for everyone else as well.

Only by following the spiritual path, permitting it to be our primary guide in life, may we find inner peace, true happiness, eternal love, and genuine meaning in our life.

It is only when we walk through life with love and humility, quietly helping others in need, the true essence of life will reveal itself.

Living in an unpredictable self-centered world of distrust, many are guarded, suspicious of others.

Though caution may be necessary, it will not be until we begin to trust others, always considering the best interests of all, rather than only ourselves, that true change may finally occur and the many challenges humanity faces begin to be mitigated.

Our thoughts, influenced by our self-centered beliefs, help determine our path through life.

They help shape our prejudices, fears, and acceptance of the status quo.

We awaken when we begin to realize these beliefs mask our true purpose in life.

We become enlightened when we understand that our purpose is to selflessly share our spirit's wisdom and unconditional love with others, so they too may realize this is their purpose in life as well.

Regardless of our differences, we are all brothers and sisters, related by a common purpose, deeply connected through a shared spirit, a piece of god present within each of us.

Only together, by selflessly sharing our spirit's wisdom and unconditional love to help each other, may we all succeed and flourish, discovering our life's genuine purpose.

Apart, regardless of our success, our life will have been lived without purpose or meaning.

Both the ego, our learned beliefs, and the spirit, our inherent source of wisdom and love, accompany every life.

Their views about life though, are diametrically opposite.

The ego's only concern is self-gratification; the spirit, however, is also worried about all others as well.

Whichever is our primary guide will determine if we discover authentic love, inner peace, true happiness, and genuine meaning in our life or if we do not.

Regardless of our circumstances in life, we each may change the direction of our life by viewing it through a different prism.

When we gaze at life through the eyes of our essence, allowing our spirit within to be our primary guide, we awaken to the possibilities life truly offers.

Doing so, our challenges, regardless of cause, lessen, as a true realization of the genuine purpose of our life's journey, to unconditionally share our wisdom, love, and excess with all others, becomes evident.

Despite our situation in life, we each decide our own destiny.

Those who choose to follow the self-centered path, concerned only for themselves, *despite* their success or accomplishments in life, are destined to live a life without meaning.

Those, however, who pursue the loving spiritual path, *regardless* of their success or failures, are destined to discover the genuine purpose for their life's journey.

Life is a gift, a spiritual journey meant to be benevolently shared to selflessly help all in need when they face challenges in their life.

This is why we are alive.

Any other belief is a myth, fostered by the ego, our learned beliefs, to challenge our life's true intention.

When we look at another, most see only their appearance.

Those, however, who have awoken, beginning to sense their loving spirit within, when they look at another, though they too see what they look like, they also sense their spirit as well.

Doing so, they are able to see past the outer layer and façade others present, to view the genuine beauty and love that has always been present within each.

Many learn to wear masks, hiding their true feelings and emotions from the world.

The mask, created by the ego, our learned beliefs, protects us from pain others may inflict on us through their words, actions, or deeds.

Hiding behind a façade, the mask also stifles the wisdom and messages of unconditional love present within each of us.

Only by ripping off our mask and embracing the messages of our spirit within, may we truly begin to discover the genuine purpose of our life's journey.

As death approaches, many begin to review the life they had led.

What they once thought was success often holds a different meaning now.

Though they may have had wealth, material possessions, family, did the best things life offers, if they did not selflessly share their success with others, their life will have been lived without meaning or purpose.

When you see another, look beyond the superficial layers and façade they project, to the essence, the spirit, within.

Only then will you truly know who they are, rather than just the illusion they project to the world.

Our destiny is to embrace the spiritual path through life, realizing every life, each with a spirit, a piece of god within, regardless of our differences, accomplishments, or genus, is equal, connected, and important.

To fulfill our destiny though, we must be willing to confront and challenge our past.

Most never realize their life's true intention; it is simply easier to continue to believe what they were taught is true.

With the reemergence of our loving spirit within, we start to retake control of our life, beginning us on a journey to reach our true destiny.

Many search for meaning in their life.

Most believe they will find it if they get a good job, make a lot of money, have a family, enjoy life.

Though they may attain their goals, meaning may not be found in a self-centered world.

It must first be discovered within, then, by discarding our false learned beliefs and embracing the wisdom and unconditional loving messages of our spirit within, we each will find meaning in our life, as the genuine purpose for our life's journey will be understood.

Never judge another by their beliefs, appearance, façade they present to the world.

Our value does not reside in any of these things.

The true worth of another lies only within, where our spirit accompanies each to selflessly share its wisdom and unconditional love with the world.

Humanity is on a spiritual journey, contained in a human shell, inside which a spirit is present to give our lives direction and meaning.

Our spirit does this by sharing its inherent wisdom and unconditional love to help guide our life's choices.

All man-made problems occur when humanity does not understand this, embracing instead its human self-centered beliefs, rather than its spiritual core.

The ego, our learned beliefs, exists to teach us how to survive in the world.

Its mandate is to protect and convince us meaning and success may be found in a self-centered world.

Though the ego is important, helping us adjust to living in the world, by blindly following its direction, our life will be led without meaning.

Only by questioning the truth of what we were taught, may we begin to understand our true purpose in life.

The ego, our self-centered beliefs, gains strength from everything we learn and believe is true, constantly struggling to dominate the direction of our life.

Though the ego is essential for our survival, it is only when its presence is diminished, allowing our spirit to become the primary guide in our life, that we may find true happiness, inner peace, and genuine meaning in our life.

Those who blindly accept the self-centered beliefs of the world are asleep, trapped in a matrix, an illusion of reality.

Only when we start to challenge these beliefs may we awaken, beginning us on a path to discover the genuine reason for our life's journey.

Many endlessly search the world seeking happiness, love, and meaning in their life.

These, though, may not be found in a self-centered world.

To find true happiness, love, and meaning, we must first look within.

They have always been there, simply waiting for our permission to be discovered.

Darkness and light accompany each of us throughout our life.

Darkness results from blindly accepting our learned self-centered beliefs.

Light symbolizes our original loving purpose, mostly forgotten, suppressed by our ego's dominance.

Only when we choose light rather than darkness, may we awaken, beginning us on a path to rediscover the genuine purpose of our life's journey.

Many desire success.

Though they may become wealthy, have many material possessions, and be able to enjoy life's many pleasures, these things will not help in discovering their life's true purpose.

To discover genuine meaning in our life, we must selflessly share our success with those less fortunate, helping them to become successful in their life as well.

Our Search for Love

Our Search for Love

Words are not necessary to reveal our love.

Gently hold another's hand, quietly listen to their reflections, warmly hug them when they need strength, look deeply into their eyes, their soul within.

Then they will truly know your love.

Open your heart.

Listen to the soft intimate whispers.

What do you hear, feel?

Love.

Everything else, every senseless harmful emotion learned after we are born, is there to challenge our choices in life.

To discover the genuine reason for your life's journey, follow the messages of your heart, then share your love unconditionally with all others.

We may choose to live our lives in fear, focusing only on our own success in the world.

Or we may live our lives with love, selflessly sharing our excess and compassion with all others.

One leads to a life of mediocrity; the other to a genuine understanding of our life's true purpose.

Gaze past the façade others present to the world.

To truly know another, look beyond their presentation, to their very soul within, sharing an intimate loving moment together, as your soul's unite as one, changing the direction of both of your lives forever.

We are all linked together by love, intimately connected to each other by a spirit, a piece of god present within each.

To discover our life's genuine purpose, open your heart, then release your infinite love, your spirit, for the benefit all.

We each choose how we see another.

Do we observe only their flaws or the infinite love present within?

Most see the former, living their life detached from others, concerned only for themselves.

For those who see the latter, however, seeing past the façade others present to the world, their life is enriched, intimately getting to know the other by uniting their loving spirit's together as one.

Every life is exceptional, beautiful in every way.

It matters not appearance, beliefs, flaws, or any other differences there may be between us.

Embrace each other with unconditional love, rather than judgment, seeing beyond the exterior and façade of another, to their loving flawless essence within.

Every person we meet affects both of our lives.

A small part of our spirit, our essence, remains within each of us.

Every one of us can therefore change the world by selflessly sharing our spirit's wisdom and unconditional love to help awaken the spirit within others.

They then, may do the same with all those they meet in their lives as well, helping to spread the circle of love around the world.

Conditional love is shared with the hope of receiving something in return.

Though many believe this is what love is, it is not.

True love is inherent, coming from within, given freely without expectation of benefit.

This pure form of love originates from our spirit, soul, god, present within every life.

Sharing our spirit's unconditional love selflessly with all others, even those we may not know or who are different from us, is the real reason for our life's journey.

Unconditional love, inherent within every life, is the most powerful force in the universe.

The love between a mother and her newborn, regardless of genus, exemplifies this pure form of love.

Selflessly sharing it, without motive or benefit, to help others rediscover their innate love as well, is the genuine purpose of our life's journey.

Shine your light brightly; share your essence, your love unconditionally with all others, spreading inner peace and love around the world.

Doing so, you may help awaken in others their spirit within as well, beginning them on a journey to discover inner peace and love in their life as well.

There are many people, though surrounded by countless others, who are alone, seeking to find love and companionship in the world.

Hiding behind a façade created to protect them when they were young, they project an artificial cloak hiding their true feelings and emotions from all others and, even from themselves.

Only when we lower our protective barrier, allowing us to genuinely open our heart, may we never be alone again and truly know what love is.

With the complete acceptance of the spiritual path, love imbues every cell of our body, surrounding us in a brilliant aura of light.

The only emotion we sense is unconditional love, desiring to share it selflessly to benefit all others.

All emotions are learned.

They do not exist until after our birth, exposure, and acceptance of the beliefs living in a self-centered world encourage.

Love, shared freely, unconditionally, is the only genuine emotion we are meant to know.

It is present within every life, waiting permission to be released.

With our consent we awaken, beginning us on a journey to understand our true purpose in life.

Genuine love arises from the spirit, a piece of god present within every life.

It is shared unconditionally, without motive or benefit, with all others.

Selflessly sharing this love not only brings meaning to our life, but to the lives of those we share it with as well.

Understanding this is the lesson we are alive to learn, the purpose of our life's journey.

We all wish to find love, happiness, inner peace, and meaning in our life.

Though we may experience these emotions briefly, changes in our life circumstances often cause them to vanish.

Enduring love, happiness, inner peace, and meaning will only manifest themselves when they are selflessly shared to benefit all others.

Unconditional love is the supreme power in the universe; every life eternally seeks it.

Love found in the world though, is often shared with the hope of benefit to ourselves.

This type of love, learned through our life experiences, is superficial.

To discover genuine love, it must first be found within, then shared, without reason or cause, with others.

Listen to the soft quiet whispers within.

Hear its messages of unconditional love, then share its love freely, selflessly, with all others.

To truly know another, listen intently to the silence in between our thoughts.

If we do, we may hear the underlying message, not disguised by our self-centered beliefs.

Instead, we may sense the authentic unconditional loving messages of the other's spirit, accompanying each of us on our journey through life.

This is who we truly are, not the pretense fostered by the façade we created to protect us from the world.

Regardless of our religion or beliefs, god has only one underlying message: selflessly sharing our unconditional love, regardless of our differences, to help all in need.

God does not tolerate hate or greed; or the needless struggles of the poor due to hunger, homelessness, prejudice.

God is love; any other belief is an illusion, fostered by a self-centered world, to justify the indifference and senseless inequities so many must endure.

Many learn to hide their genuine emotions, their inherent love, behind a façade they create to protect them from pain others may inflict on them.

This leads to loneliness, isolating them, not only from truly loving another, but from knowing and loving themselves as well.

Many live their entire life asleep, believing their emotions are real; they are not.

Only our core emotions, arising from our spirit within, shared without motive or benefit, are genuine.

Embracing and selflessly sharing our spirit's unconditional love with others will not only mitigate our loneliness, but also will allow us to intimately know and truly love another as well.

A single act of unconditional love shared with another may awaken in them their love as well.

By selflessly sharing our love with others, without motive or benefit, we can amplify our love exponentially, as that person may then share their love with the next, ad infinitum.

To bring genuine change to a self-centered world, perhaps we may each begin by simply sharing a single act of love.

Many view beauty by the outward appearance of another.

Genuine beauty, however, resides not on the outside.

It lies only within, where the exquisite presence and unconditional love of another has always been.

We are born radiating a blinding aura, knowing only unconditional love.

Our glow begins to dim when we accept the many false self-centered beliefs we learn, as we are socialized to accept society's norms.

We then often spend the rest of our life trying to rediscover our light's brilliance once more.

Our words and actions may affect the lives of every person we interact with.

A single incident may have a profound effect on someone for the rest of their life.

Therefore always treat all others with kindness, compassion, and unconditional love, ushering in a new era, a spiritual evolution, for humanity.

All learned emotions, both positive and negative, are an illusion.

Though they may seem real, they are not.

Unconditional love, inherent within every life, selflessly shared to benefit others, is the only genuine emotion.

To truly know another, gaze past their façade to their loving essence within.

When we primarily lead our life following our heart rather than our mind, the beauty of the world reveals itself in innumerable ways.

Love, present within every life, is shared unconditionally, making life easier, more meaningful, for both ourselves and those we sincerely share our love with.

Choose to follow the more challenging path through life, the path of the heart, opening your world to discovering genuine happiness, infinite love, and true meaning in your life as well.

Would we approach life differently if we knew death was imminent? Our wealth, possessions, accomplishments, will not accompany us when we die.

All that will remain is our unconditional love, our spirit, remaining within all those we selflessly shared it with, intimately merging our spirit with theirs.

To live a truly meaningful life, do not wait not until death approaches to share your love.

Share your love every day without motive or benefit.

When you do, you will not only discover genuine love in your life, but also inner peace and meaning as well.

~ *326* ~

The meaning of life is not difficult to understand.

It is to selflessly share our spirit's wisdom and unconditional love with all others, including those who are different from us.

When we do, we remind them to share their love with others as well and each of us becomes stronger and our journey through life less challenging and more meaningful.

Helping each other by selflessly sharing our unconditional love, our spirit with all others, even those we may not know, is how life is meant to be lived.

Only then may our hearts begin to soften, allowing us to start on a path to understand the reason we are alive.

Our body is but a vessel to contain our spirit within.

Our self-centered beliefs, reflected by our actions, thoughts, and deeds, do not mirror who we genuinely are either.

To discover who another truly is, gaze beyond what you see and the façade they present to the world, to their genuine loving soul within.

For this is who we truly are.

Our prose may arise from our mind or from the inherent loving emotions within our heart.

When they come from our mind, our words are often influenced by our self-centered beliefs and experiences in life.

When they come from our heart, however, words are not necessary; a simple touch, loving look, warm embrace, intimately connects us to another more than our words could ever express.

All, without exception, have flaws, as a result of accepting the false beliefs we were taught when we learned to survive in a self-centered world.

When another harms us, look beyond the injury to the authentic person behind their flawed façade.

Only then may we truly be able to discard the pain, replacing it with understanding, compassion, and unconditional love in its stead.

See only the best in others.

Ignore the disguise they present to the world.

When we do, all that remains is love.

We are light, spirit, knowing only unconditional love, possessing the wisdom of the universe within.

With our birth, however, the ego, our learned beliefs, is formed, darkening our understanding of our life's true purpose.

To return to the pure bright light we once knew, we must confront our self-centered beliefs, realizing they are inhibiting us from finding the answers about life we seek.

Our words may spread love, but they may also be the cause of great pain.

Hurtful words may cause trauma, at times affecting someone for the entirety of their life.

Even one encounter may genuinely aid or terribly harm another.

Our life's purpose is to help not hurt, love not hate other's.

Our words, therefore, must always reflect kindness, compassion, and be shared with unconditional love.

When we awaken, sensing the first quiet messages from our spirit within, instead of seeing only the worse in others, we now begin to see the best.

Instead of darkness, we see light.

And instead of accepting living in a world of fear, we now wish to change the world, so we may all live in a world of love instead.

Everyone desires love in their life.

Those who seek to find love in a self-centered world, though they may fleetingly experience it, that feeling often disappears with our changing life circumstances.

To find true love, it must first be found within.

Then, it will only truly be experienced by sharing your love, your spirit, selflessly with all others, so they too may experience love in their life as well.

"Raising Our Children With Love"

~ 336 ~

The first time a child sees the world, their eyes are wide open.

The child has only one emotion in its heart: unconditional love meant to be shared without cause with all others.

Differences matter not, inherently knowing every life, regardless of form or distinctions, is equally important, each having a spirit, a piece of god within.

As they begin to learn about the self-centered world though, their eyes begin to close.

They then may spend the rest of their life struggling, as they try to awaken and completely reopen their eyes once more.

When we raise our children to embrace tolerance rather than prejudice, generosity rather than selfishness, and love rather than fear, they need not spend the rest of their life undoing the harm done during their most impressionable years.

For these children will discover true happiness, inner peace, authentic love, and live their lives with genuine purpose and meaning.

When a young child sees the world for the first time, they see a world of endless possibilities; a world where there is hope, love, and compassion.

They have not yet learned to be cynical, prejudiced, self-centered, though it does not take long before their lessons begin.

To truly change the direction of the world, we all need to remember and embrace the world as it could be when we first saw it through the eyes of a young child.

Living in a dysfunctional world where violence, prejudice, inequity, hunger exist, our children grow up accepting humanity's darkness as a normal part of life.

Children are innocent, meant to play, enjoy life, embrace the love and purity it offers.

They are meant to live in a world of peace, love, and light.

Only when humanity adopts the loving spiritual path through life, instead of the self-centered path it has always followed, may our children finally be able to live in such a world.

The earliest years in a child's life often determines their beliefs, prejudices, and overall view of the world.

During these years, a child will learn to either accept the views of a self-centered world, emphasizing only what is best for themself, or they will learn to be equally concerned for all others as well.

Though both are necessary and important to know, it is only when a child is raised to primarily embrace the loving spiritual path through life, realizing the importance of every life regardless of our differences, that they may be well adjusted and discover inner peace, enduring love, and genuine meaning in their life as well.

We all wish our children to be happy during their life.

If a child is raised to believe happiness may only be experienced if they have money, material possessions, a family, even if they achieve all their goals, they will never know what true happiness is.

This type of happiness is fleeting, often disappearing with life's challenges, never enduring in a self-centered world.

True happiness may only be discovered when it is first found within, then it must be selflessly shared with all others to help them discover happiness in their life as well.

Raise our children to live their lives with love rather than hate, compassion rather than apathy, acceptance rather than prejudice; to willingly share their unconditional love with others, rather than only to worry about themselves.

If we do, our children may then change the world, allowing humanity to further its spiritual evolution.

Imagine a world where our children are brought up to embrace the wisdom and unconditional love of the spirit, the piece of god present within each life.

They would know compassion, empathy, and the importance of treating everyone and every life, regardless of our differences, with respect, kindness, and love.

Though they must learn about the dangers of living in a self-centered world, our children would instead be raised in a world where love is freely, unconditionally shared for the betterment of all, and where hate, fear, and greed are simply memories of the past.

Children are born innocent, knowing only unconditional love, understanding every life, regardless of our differences or genus, is important, equal, and connected.

They realize their purpose in life is to selflessly share their wisdom and love, their spirit, without motive or benefit, with all others.

With our birth, however, the ego, our self-centered beliefs, is created as we are taught how to survive and succeed in a self-centered world.

If we raise our children in their formative years to primarily embrace love rather than fear, they will grow up well-adjusted, happy, and live a life of meaning, rather than one of relentless struggle.

Our children are needlessly dying, their light extinguished before their appointed time.

Innocent, they die from indiscriminate violence, drugs, starvation, their slight bodies lifeless in an uncaring world, too self-centered to care or notice.

A world allowing the genocide of children is untenable.

To end this carnage, we must rise up, challenge the self-absorbed beliefs allowing this to happen, then embrace all our children, regardless of their appearance, beliefs, or circumstances in life, with unconditional love and genuine concern for their well-being, rather than to continue to feign ignorance and indifference to the injustices they may suffer in the world.

Our children are born innocent.

They soon lose their naiveite though, as they are exposed to living in a self-centered world of inequity and indifference.

As they are growing up, they observe people starving, homeless, dying from senseless violence; they also learn about hate, prejudice, and the needless struggles others endure.

Their innocence, once pure with their birth, now is forever tainted.

To allow our children to return to their innocence, humanity must learn to embrace love rather than fear, being equally concerned for the importance of every life, rather than only for their own.

If humanity does not soon change its self-centered beliefs, our children will inherit a world of indifference, prejudice, inequity; of endless violence, hunger, homelessness, as they mature into adulthood.

Change would require humanity to be equally concerned for each other, all lifeforms, and our planet itself, rather than only for themselves.

If we truly love our children and want to improve the future they may have to confront, how can we not embrace this change now, before it is no longer possible.

The numerous struggles we may have throughout our life often result from the many false self-centered beliefs we are taught during our early impressionable years when we are children.

We then may spend the rest of our life confronting these falsehoods, endlessly battling to undo the damage these beliefs caused.

Parents may prevent many of the struggles our children may face later in their life, simply by raising them with love rather than fear.

It they do, these children will then learn to treat all others, regardless of their differences, with respect and kindness, and view life with wonder and awe, rather than fear and distrust.

How much is our children's future worth, allowing them to grow up in a world better than the one we have created and live in?

Humanity has the ability now to mitigate almost every manmade challenge.

What prevents this from happening is greed and the blind acceptance of the self-centered status quo.

Only by realizing the equal importance of every life and sharing our resources and excess equitably, may our children's future be brighter, allowing love and peace on earth to become our new reality.

As children, we are taught our value in the world and superiority to not only all other forms of life, but to others who are different from us as well.

Since we are new to this world, we believe and accept everything we are told.

Imagine instead, if we raised our children to love all others, rather than fear them, to selflessly help others, rather than ignore them, and to recognize the equal importance of every life, rather than being only concerned about what is best for ourself.

In this world, our children will live with peace, love, and light, rather than continue to have to live in a world of war, hate, and darkness.

Children should know joy.

Instead they know pain, observing the many challenges they and others must face resulting from living in a self-centered world.

They see children and others needlessly die from starvation, random violence, indifference; struggle from homelessness, hunger, prejudice.

The only way to mitigate our children's pain is to embrace unconditional love instead of hate, helping all who are struggling regardless of their appearance, beliefs, or circumstances in life.

Only then may our children grow up knowing happiness rather than sorrow, as they were always meant to do.

If the world were led by children, there would be no prejudice, hate, war, hunger.

Our children inherently understand helping and loving each other is better than harming and hating another.

They realize every person who is struggling should be aided in their time of need.

They see not the color of another's skin, nor they do they differentiate others due to their religion, ethnicity, wealth, or any other differences there may be.

Perhaps our world would be better if we listened to our spiritually advanced children, rather than the adults who simply perpetuate the status quo.

Our children are taught and encouraged to accept the self-centered beliefs of the world.

They learn about prejudice, inequity, and the value of worrying only about themselves, while ignoring the struggles of others.

If we raised our children with love rather than fear, to selflessly care and help each other, they would then be able to live in a world of tolerance, compassion, and peace instead.

To raise happy well-adjusted children, teach them to find their path
and happiness not in the self-centered world, but from their
spirit within instead, then to selflessly share their spirit's wisdom and
unconditional love, without motive or benefit, with all others.

The first five years of a child's life are the most important.

It is then they will form their opinions, prejudices, beliefs, and aspirations about the world and those who live in it.

If we raise our children during these years to treat everyone with love, kindness, and compassion, understanding every life, regardless of our differences, is equally important, they may then be able to live in a world of love, rather than fear.

Darkness & Light:

The World We Line IN

Darkness & Light:

The World We Live In

We each choose whether we will build a wall or a bridge.

The wall isolates us, not only from each other, but from ourselves as well.

Rather than dividing us, the bridge connects all life to each other.

If we view the world through a wall, having only a partial view of it as we gaze over its top, we will only see a superficial image, a façade we each project to others.

When we see a world full of bridges though, we will sense the wisdom and unconditional love that is present within each, intimately connecting us to each other, wishing only to help all others we see on the other side of the bridge instead.

How we view the world depends on the eyes through which we see it.

If we accept all we were taught, the world will be a very dark place, its colors muted by an array of impure hues.

If, however, the world is seen through the eyes of our loving spirit, soul, god, within, our vision will become clear revealing the infinite possibilities life offers.

Most accept the status quo, believing all they learned about how to survive and be happy in a self-centered world.

It is a world of greed, prejudice, inequity; of war, hunger, homelessness.

It takes courage to challenge the accepted norms and beliefs of the majority.

Every person though, can change the world, mitigating many of humanity's man-made challenges and harmful actions.

We each have always had within us the means to do so.

It begins by listening quietly, accepting the wisdom and loving messages you hear, then sharing your inherent light, your unconditional love, with the world.

Blindly accepting the beliefs of the world, many waste their lives pursuing fictitious dreams of success and happiness.

Nothing we were taught or accomplish in a self-centered world will allow us to find either genuine success or true happiness.

These may only be found within, by embracing the innate wisdom and unconditional loving messages of our spirit, then must be selflessly shared with others, so they too may find success and happiness in their lives as well.

Humanity may choose to live in a world of fear, worrying only about themselves, or in a world of unconditional love, worrying equally about every life as well.

The former will lead to the continuation of the status quo; the latter to the spiritual evolution of our species.

Only if we choose to live in a world of love rather than fear may our planet survive and our children, and all life on it thrive.

If we do nothing, the choice may soon be made for us.

By selflessly sharing our wisdom and unconditional love to improve the life of all on our planet, we each may change the world.

Our warmth will bring light to an indifferent world, one often embracing darkness.

Doing so may also reawaken a long dormant memory in another to life's genuine possibilities.

We each view the world differently, seeing a variety of hues depending on the day.

Some days everything appears hazy, blurred by stress, anxiety, and struggle.

Other days, though, we see a world that is luminous and transparent.

To see clarity and the pure unobstructed colors of the world, selflessly share your wisdom and unconditional love, your spirit, with others, thereby easing their burdens in life, allowing them to begin to see the vibrant colors of the world as well.

Seeing the needless struggles of so many, wishing to help, we do not, becoming exhausted, indifferent, apathetic, believing there is little we may do to bring lasting change.

We therefore accept these events as an inevitable part of life; they are not.

Though we are tired, we must not abandon those most in need, rejecting the accepted status quo of indifference.

Only then may humanity spiritually evolve, and the future of our planet and all who inhabit it, be assured.

Humanity has never been superior, though they believe they are.

While they are the dominant species on our planet, allowing them to take advantage of lower life forms, the earth, and each other, this belief is the reason humanity remains in its spiritual infancy.

Only by truly respecting the equal importance of every life, the symbiotic relationship mankind has with all lifeforms, our planet, and each other, may humanity evolve, allowing them to discover their true purpose in the universe.

Our children will inherit a world of violence, hunger, poverty; of greed, prejudice, inequity.

Not one of these man-made challenges or emotions need exist.

They are only present due to humanity's acceptance of the self-centered status quo.

To change this paradigm, allowing our children to live in a world of peace, love, and equality, humanity must embrace a new path through life; one where every life, regardless of their differences or accomplishments, is equally valued, treated with respect and empathy, and selflessly helped in their time of need.

Imagine a world influenced by the spirit within; a world of unconditional love, hope, equality, empathy, and peace, rather than a world of fear, hate, prejudice, distrust, and inequity.

We each may choose which world we will live in.

By embracing the spiritual path, selflessly sharing our spirit's wisdom and love unconditionally with all, we each may change the world, allowing our planet to begin to heal and our children to be able to live in a world of love and peace, rather than to continue to live in a world of hate and conflict.

Greed is the cause of poverty, homelessness, hunger, and many of humanity's self-inflicted problems.

Rather than sharing our resources equally to help all in need, the wealthy and powerful dictate humanity's continuing inequities and struggles.

To rid the world of greed, there must be a paradigm shift, embracing the belief what is best for everyone is more important than what is best just for the few.

Dream of a world where love is freely shared; there is no hunger, prejudice, war, inequity.

A world where none of the innumerable problems and harmful emotions define our existence.

To make such a dream reality, we each must decide to embrace empathy over indifference, generosity over greed, and love over fear.

We do not know the many challenges someone has faced in their life; therefore we have no right to judge another.

All we may do is be there for them, sharing our spirit, our love unconditionally, to try to ease their burden and journey through life.

By seeing the world through a prism of light rather than darkness, we may change the course of not only their life, but of the world itself.

It is our choice how we view the world and those who live in it.

It has little to do with our upbringing, wealth, race, religion, or anything else we learned about as we were brought up to accept society's self-centered beliefs.

To live a life of meaning, choose to see light rather than darkness, then share your radiant spark, your spirit, with the world.

Humanity focuses only on their own survival and success in the world, without concern for other forms of life, the planet we live on, or each other.

Instead of selflessly helping each other, as life is meant to be lived, we care only about ourselves.

To change this paradigm, making the world safer for our children to live in, we must always consider what is best for everyone, rather than only for ourselves.

~ *372* ~

Religion, created by man, divides the world; spirituality unites it.

Though religion may have begun with good intentions, its interpretations of its basic tenets soon took on human meanings.

The result of this is war, prejudice, inequity, due to humanity's different beliefs about god.

Spirituality comes from within, where the inherent loving beliefs and wisdom of god, spirit, soul, exists in every life.

These are the pure whole emotions and beliefs we are meant to share with all others.

Everyone, regardless of their religion or differences, are equally accepted; no one religion is considered better than another.

Instead, the loving messages and wisdom of our spirit are selflessly shared to benefit all.

Humanity justifies many of the horrific events happening in the world, caused by greed, prejudice, inequity, as a normal part of life.

Believing they cannot change what is happening, they dehumanize those experiencing these atrocities, convincing themselves the life of those who are suffering is not as important as theirs's.

It is only when humanity begins to realize, regardless of our differences, we must never ignore any who are struggling and in need, may our world awaken, allowing its spiritual evolution to truly begin.

Though technology has made life easier, without the spiritual evolution of humanity, its inevitable decline will barely cause a ripple in our vast galaxy.

Though many souls will perish, life will continue undeterred elsewhere in the universe.

Only by selflessly supporting each other may our planet begin to heal, allowing our children a chance to live in a world of unconditional love, rather than to continue to live in a world of endless fear.

The lie begins with our birth, when we are taught to accept and inflate our importance in the world, not only to lower forms of life, but to each other as well.

The lie is the cause of prejudice, greed, inequity, and all of humanity's harmful self-centered beliefs and emotions.

Only when we realize we have never been better or more important than any other, will these destructive beliefs start to abate, allowing our world to begin to heal.

Fear is the underlying cause of hate, prejudice, inequity, resulting in a world of needless deaths, violence, hunger, and all of humanity's unnecessary struggles.

Only when we embrace love rather than fear, accepting the inherent good, rather than the flawed within every life, may we be able to begin to break this relentless cycle, ushering in a new spiritual age for humanity.

We all have moments in life when stress and our emotions affect how we react in the world.

In times of balance, we are steady.

There are periods in our life, however, our reactions may be extreme.

During these times, we may calm our response by embracing our spirit's wisdom, allowing love to dictate our reply rather than fear.

Every generation, when they are young, believe they are going to change the world.

For most, as they get older and have more responsibilities, reality encourages them to accept society's illusions.

They soon forget about their dreams, settling into a life of mediocrity, seeking their happiness, success, and answers in a self-centered world; they may not be found there.

To bring genuine change in the world, we must remember what we once believed when we were young and idealistic.

Only together, by challenging humanity's many self-inflicted problems and harmful emotions, and sharing our love unconditionally with all others, will true change happen, allowing the world to evolve and peace on earth to flourish.

Humanity has the ability now to feed the hungry, clothe and house the needy, end intolerance, and many of their other self-inflicted challenges.

The inequities result from the acceptance of our self-centered beliefs, allowing the greed of the few and powerful to dictate the unnecessary struggles of others.

We must no longer accept these things as an irrefutable part of life.

It is time to alter this paradigm by embracing the loving messages and wisdom of our spirit within, then equally sharing our excess for the benefit of all.

Every life, regardless of our differences, beliefs, or genus, is sacred.

It matters not what form or appearance that life is.

Each has a spirit, a piece of god within, inextricably connecting us to each other.

Only by embracing our similarities, rather than our differences, understanding there is a symbiotic relationship existing between each life, will humanity, our planet, and all life on it, thrive.

Apart, we will each fail.

Humanity is a cult, blindly following the preaching of those who are wealthy or in authority, deciding the future for all others.

This cult is predicated on accepting our self-centered beliefs, determining how we will live our life and judge others in the world.

The only way to free ourselves from this cult is to embrace our loving spiritual center, present within every life, then selflessly share its wisdom and love unconditionally with all others, so they too may begin to free themselves from this cult as well.

There are many who seek their answers in the world believing religion, wealth, material possessions, will provide them; they will not.

What most are looking for may never be found in a self-centered world.

The answers they seek may only be found by fully embracing the wisdom and unconditional loving guidance of the spirit within.

When we sincerely do so, the genuine answers about life's meaning will be understood.

Living in a spiritual world, we would freely help each other, reach out when others are down, help pick them up, and gently assist them to stand on their own once again.

This world, after its spiritual evolution, is the loving world we were always meant to live in.

Humanity must choose between two futures.

The first choice there is war, hunger, prejudice, inequity.

The other choice, a spiritually evolved world, there would be cooperation, love, equality, ridding the world of many of its man-made harmful choices.

The only question we must ask ourselves is: which future will we choose for our children to inherit?

When we were young, we were idealistic; we were going to change the world.

As we got older though, trying to succeed and find happiness, our enthusiasm began to wane, our idealism began to fade.

We eventually accepted society's self-centered definition of success and happiness, concerned only for ourselves, rather than worrying about others.

It is not too late though, to open our hearts and selflessly share our inherent love and wisdom to benefit others.

Doing so, we may change the direction of the world, making it better for our children and each other.

Continuing to live in a world of conflict and innumerable man-made challenges, as long as humanity's focus remains isolated on itself, on only what is best for them and not others, nothing will change.

Life will continue as it has until the earth is barren.

Only by embracing the loving spiritual path, being equally concerned for each other, every form of life, and our planet itself, may our world thrive, and may enduring peace replace endless conflict, and unconditional love replace the many unnecessary challenges resulting from humanity's self-centered beliefs.

Humanity treats each other, other forms of life, and our planet as insignificant, unimportant.

Most are only concerned about themself, ignoring the struggles of others.

Unless genuine change is embraced, a new path forged, one that cares equally for every life, regardless of our differences or genus, the deteriorating future for humanity, all other forms of life, and our world itself, may no longer be able to be changed.

Regardless of the provocation, there is never just cause to harm another.

It matters not if the injury is physical, verbal, or in any other manner.

Only by treating each other, regardless of our differences, with kindness rather than malice, may our world begin to evolve, allowing our children to grow up in a world of love, rather than hate.

We live in a dysfunctional self-centered world, allowing many to struggle due to humanity's indifference.

Though most man-made challenges may be ended today, we choose not to.

Rather humanity prefers to accept the status quo.

Inequity, prejudice, war, hunger, are but a few of the hundreds of problems and harmful actions we ignore, believing there is little we may do to stop these injustices.

We may end these needless hardships though.

To do so, humanity must wake from its slumber, realizing only together, recognizing the equal importance of every life, will our planet and all life on it thrive, and humanity's many self-inflicted problems be mitigated.

Though humanity is the dominant species on our planet, its life is no more meaningful than any other.

Only together, realizing the equal importance and symbiotic relationship humanity has with all forms of life, each other, and our planet itself, may they evolve and the future of our planet be assured.

There are those who consider money more important than people.

Though we have the technology and ability to rid our planet of hunger, homelessness, climate change, and many of the other man-made scourges now, we instead choose to accept these things as a normal part of life.

By challenging the status quo and everything we learned and believed to be true, we can renounce the ideology of competition and self-interest, replacing it instead with universal concern for all.

We sit idly by while our children senselessly die from war, hunger, drugs, random violence.

A society that does not protect its children is immoral.

The only cure for this apathy and indifference, to stop the genocide that is caused by greed, prejudice, inequity, is to denounce the self-centered status quo, realizing it is the cause of our children's early demise.

Instead, we must recognize the equal importance of every child's life, regardless of their differences or circumstances in life.

Only then, may our children be able to survive and live in a world of love rather than fear.

Our planet's existence in the vast universe is insignificant, like a grain of sand on a beach, or a drop of water in a massive ocean.

If humanity does not spiritually evolve, learning to equally love, respect, and care about every life despite our many differences, our world will simply become another lifeless planet in a universe too grand to care or remember.

Many believe it is humanity's nature to kill each other, be self-centered, take advantage of others for their own benefit.

Nothing could be further from the truth.

We have simply forgotten our true nature, which has always been to sincerely care about each other, selflessly help all in need, and to share our love unconditionally with all others.

Living in a self-centered world, conflict, both in the world and within each of us, is inevitable.

Almost every conflict in the world is preventable, caused by greed and the acceptance of the status quo.

Conflict within, however, may result from the struggle between what we were taught and believe to be true and what is and always has been the truth.

By embracing the spirit, rather than the ego as our primary guide through life, much of the conflict, both in the world and within us may be resolved, being replaced with inner peace, unconditional love, and a true understanding of our life's purpose.

We live in a self-centered world, worrying only about what is best for ourself.

It is a world of inequity, allowing many to live in poverty, struggling every day to find food to eat, clothes to wear, shelter to protect them from the elements.

In a spiritual world, following the unconditional loving guidance and wisdom of our spirit within, we realize the equal importance of every life.

In this world, each would be selflessly helped in their time of need.

Humanity has the ability now, by equally distributing our resources and sincerely caring about each other, to end many of these hardships today.

They do not, however, because the greed of the few and powerful have convinced the rest this is normal; it is not and never has been.

There are those in the world who are invisible, ignored by society.

They may be homeless, poor, mentally challenged, a minority; the reason matters not.

Every life, regardless of their circumstances, is, and has always been, equally important, deserving to be helped when life challenges them.

In a spiritual world, no one is invisible, realizing life will only be meaningful when we all succeed together, allowing each of us to live a life of true meaning and purpose.

Any problem solved in the world is temporary, until those with influence cause it to return once more.

Though we can rid the world of hunger, homelessness, climate change now, unless we fix the underlying cause, the acceptance of the self-centered beliefs of the world, little will change.

Before we can truly transform the world, we must first change ourselves, by embracing the wisdom and messages of unconditional love present within each of us, then selflessly sharing them to benefit all others.

Only then will equity and compassion replace greed and indifference, allowing everyone, not just the few, to find abundance in their life as well.

There are many who believe those who are wealthy, famous, have a prestigious job, deserve their excess, while others, struggling every day to find food to eat, shelter to keep them safe, do not.

Believing some, due to their accomplishments, race, ethnicity, are superior to those who are different or less fortunate, divides our world endlessly.

Only by selflessly sharing our excess and love, equally helping all in need, regardless of our differences, may our world evolve, mitigating the struggles so many needlessly endure.

We are all part of a whole, each having a symbiotic relationship to the other; harming one, causes injury to all.

Though we appear, act, believe differently than each other, we are truly one, linked by a common bond, a spirit, a piece of god within, divided only by our outward differences and beliefs.

To allow any part to fail will result in universal loss for all.

Do not gaze away from those less fortunate, trying to ignore their pain.

We must no longer disregard those who are struggling, allowing them to go unnoticed.

This is our true purpose in life, to selflessly help those in need by sharing our wisdom and unconditional love, our spirit, to benefit others.

Imagine a world where we equally shared our resources and love; no one would be without shelter, hungry, alone.

All decisions would be made collectively, always considering what is best for all, rather than just for one.

In this world no one, regardless of their differences or accomplishments, would be considered better or more important than another.

This is what living in an enlightened world is like, cooperating rather than competing, sincerely caring about each other, rather than worrying only about ourselves.

This is what our world can look like after humanity's spiritual evolution.

This is the world we are meant to live in.

We live in a world where the greed of the few outweighs the needs of the many; where money is more important than people or the planet we live on.

Only when humanity realizes the insanity of these beliefs, recognizing the importance of our planet and all life on it, may true change finally occur.

Many people believe power comes from wealth, having an important job, from the world.

It does not.

Genuine power may only truly be experienced by reuniting with our spirit within, then selflessly sharing its wisdom and unconditional love to benefit all others.

Every person has a physical body, conscious mind, and spiritual soul.

Simply observe the world both today and throughout history to see what ignoring the spiritual soul may lead to.

War, hunger, homelessness; prejudice, greed, inequity, have dominated humanity's brief existence on earth.

Only when the spiritual soul is recognized and its path followed, may these and all of humanity's many self-imposed challenges be mitigated and the future of our planet and all life on it be assured.

Most surrender, accepting the world as it is, believing little may be done to change or improve life on our planet.

Our indifference results in needless deaths from war, hunger, disease; needless struggles from greed, prejudice, inequity.

This view, though, is predicated on a false premise, learned as we were taught how to survive in a self-centered world.

Change is possible, though we must first transform ourselves by accepting the spiritual path through life, then sharing its innate wisdom and unconditional love for the benefit of all.

Humanity has a symbiotic relationship with the earth.

Though our planet nourishes and sustains all who inhabit it, mankind treats our world with contempt, polluting its waters, fouling its skies, destroying its land, allowing many species to become extinct.

Although our planet will survive our indifference, our species may no longer grace its soil.

Humanity chooses to believe human beings are good and, when given a choice, will do the right thing.

Living in a self-centered world, however, concerned only for what is best for ourselves rather than others, this altruistic view of the world often is not reality.

Genuine change may only occur when the loving beliefs of the spirit are accepted as more important than the egoistic beliefs we have always embraced.

Living in a world dominated by fear, we worry only about what is best for us, rather than others.

The results of living in such a world are unending conflicts, anxiety, inequity, resulting in innumerable struggles for many.

We may choose at any time, however, to live in a world of love instead.

In this world, concern for every person would be more important than only for ourself, all resources and excess would be equally shared, and the many manmade problems caused the acceptance of humanity's self-centered beliefs, would be mitigated.

There are some, wishing to prove their superiority to others who think their life, due to their race, ethnicity, wealth, prestige, or any of hundreds of other comparisons, is more important than another's.

This self-centered view of the world is the cause of many of humanity's self-imposed problems and harmful beliefs.

Only by recognizing the equal value of every life, regardless of our differences or accomplishments, may our world evolve and the future for our children, and all life on our planet, be assured.

Some view the world through a negative lens, seeing only the worst in others.

They embrace society's self-centered beliefs, resulting in prejudice, inequity, struggle, and the many other challenges caused by humanity's indifference.

To break this destructive cycle of despair, we must begin to see the world through a positive lens instead, realizing only together, selflessly sharing our excess and love to help others succeed, may we all not only survive, but discover the genuine reason for our life's journey as well.

Due to the greed and power of the few, humanity is assaulting the earth, destroying its land, water, air, causing the extinction of many lower forms of life and each other.

Since mankind is intelligent and the dominant species on our world, they believe they are entitled to rape our planet.

To stop this assault, we must all wake up, be equally concerned for the well-being of the earth and every life on it, rather than only to continue to worry about what is best for ourselves.

There are some laws, especially those against causing grievous harm, that are necessary for society to function.

Many other laws, though, often reflect the will of the few, to benefit themselves, at the expense of the rest.

There is a third type of law, however, that must take precedence over all other laws: spiritual law.

The only premise of spiritual law is not doing harm to another.

It matters not if the injury is physical, verbal, emotional, or if it is from ignoring the struggles of those who are hungry, cold, in danger.

All man-made laws opposing this perspective must be challenged.

Only then, by sincerely treating each other with love rather than distrust, may our world truly evolve.

Whenever an avoidable tragedy occurs, humanity's response is often to offer thoughts and prayers for those affected.

Though these may help some, it is up to all of us to end the senseless plague of indifference caused by living in a self-centered world, concerned only for ourselves, rather than others.

We may only do this when we awaken, accepting the spirit, rather than the ego, as our primary guide in life, assuring these preventable tragedies no longer occur.

Humanity learns to judge others from a young age, believing their skin color, religion, ethnicity, wealth, or any number of other differences, make some inferior to others.

This is the cause of prejudice and many of mankind's self-inflicted challenges.

Regardless of our differences or accomplishments, no one is, or ever has been, better, their life more important than another's.

It is only when humanity truly understands this that our world may finally begin its spiritual evolution.

Since humanity is the dominant species on our planet, they believe they have certain rights bestowed on them.

They have the right to be concerned only for themself, rather than share their wealth and excess equally, so all may survive.

They have the right to needlessly kill lower forms of life and each other.

They have the right to pollute the air, water, land.

Only when humanity truly realizes every life, regardless of their differences or genus, and the earth itself, have a symbiotic relationship, needing each other to survive, may these human rights be mitigated and may our world, and all who inhabit it, thrive.

The list of humanity's self-inflicted problems is vast.

War, climate change, hunger; prejudice, inequity, greed, are but a few.

Though we may find temporary solutions to these problems, unless the underlying cause is addressed, they will forever return.

The primary motive has always been humanity's acceptance of living in a self-centered world, focused only on their own survival, rather than those who may be struggling.

To end this perpetual cycle of despair, we must embrace the wisdom and unconditional loving beliefs of our spirit within, then selflessly aid all in need.

Humanity's apathy and indifference is the reason our planet and all life on it are endangered.

Feeling there is little we may do to effect genuine change, most do nothing, surrendering to the self-centered status quo.

Every one of us may change the world.

By equally sharing our excess and our innate wisdom and unconditional love, our spirit present within each, we may each help change the future, allowing all life to thrive and our planet begin to heal.

By allowing humanity's self-inflicted problems to continue unabated, the world we are leaving our children to inherit is unimaginable.

If we do not begin to make the necessary changes now, remaining concerned only for ourselves and not our children's future, there is only one possible outcome: a continuation and worsening of the many struggles present today.

If, however, we truly care about the world our children will receive, we must begin to transform ourselves now and change the world before it is too late.

Alone we are each fragile.

Concerned only for ourselves, we ignore the needs of our planet, each other, and all life inhabiting it.

Together though, equally concerned for each, we are powerful, allowing all to thrive.

The genesis of the earth, created billions of years ago, was followed by the creation of sentient life and evolution.

As our planet rapidly approaches an abyss, a new beginning is desperately needed.

Technology alone will not solve this problem.

Only by genuinely caring for every life and our planet itself and making sacrifices for the benefit of all, may a new genesis happen, allowing the earth, and all life on it, to survive and live together in peace and harmony.

Most view the world through a dark lens, fearful of acknowledging the senseless struggles and inequities harming so many.

As the tint on our lens begins to lighten. we start to question if we may challenge the injustices by helping those needlessly suffering.

When we begin to do so, we start on a journey to understand our genuine life's purpose.

Our world, due to humanity's indifference and self-centered beliefs, is on a precipice.

Only by embracing our loving spiritual core may we mitigate the devastating effects we have had on our planet and all its inhabitants.

If we do nothing, continuing to follow the status quo, we may be unable to avoid descending into a bottomless abyss.

Human beings are arrogant, believing, due to their superior intellect, they may decide the future for all.

This arrogance is the cause of prejudice, war, inequity, and many of humanity's self-inflicted problems and challenges.

In truth, no one life, regardless of our differences, accomplishments, or genus, is, or ever has better, more important than another's.

Every life, each with a spirit, a piece of god within, is equally important.

Any other belief is arrogant.

Human beings, being the dominant most intelligent species on our planet, have an obligation to do what is best for all forms of life and our planet itself.

Only by discarding our self-centered beliefs of entitlement, embracing instead the loving inherent beliefs of our spirit within, may our responsibilities be met and our world begin to heal from the many hardships humanity has wrought on it.

Pollution, violence, hunger, extinct species, are but a few of the hundreds of challenges caused by mankind's indifference.

Only by adopting the spiritual path, selflessly sharing our excess and unconditional love with all others may genuine change occur.

If we do nothing, the choice may be soon be made for us.

Our world is at a precipice, overlooking a cavernous abyss.

The threats and problems on our planet, resulting from humanity's indifference to other forms of life, each other, and our planet itself, are almost insurmountable.

This existential moment in history may only be averted by embracing the loving spiritual path through life, being as concerned for our planet and all others as we are for ourselves.

If humanity continues to follow the status quo, they may be unable to step back from the void in time.

Humanity's destructive self-centered values and beliefs are the cause of numerous challenges causing immense damage to our planet and all who inhabit it.

If we continue on our current path, all life and the earth itself, may pay the ultimate price.

Though more people are awakening to the spiritual path, sensing the wisdom and unconditional loving messages from their spirit within, it will take a monumental shift of consciousness to mitigate our uncertain future.

In a spiritual world, everyone, regardless of our differences or accomplishments in the world, would be equally respected, helped, loved.

Our excess would be shared so every person may survive, permitting each to discover true love, inner peace, and meaning in their life.

Humanity chooses to live in a world of fear.

Violence, prejudice, inequity, are a normal part of life in this world, resulting in the unrelenting slaughter and disparate inequalities affecting so many.

It is a choice, though, to live our lives like this.

By embracing love, inherent within every life, instead of fear, the needless deaths and struggles of others may be mitigated and the future for our planet be assured.

Humanity's indifference and self-centered view of life are the cause of many of its manmade challenges.

Though we may mitigate prejudice, inequity, hunger, climate change, and every other problem resulting from living in such a world today, humanity chooses instead to make excuses, justifying their continuation.

It is time to stop defending these behaviors, rationalizing the reasons they occur.

If we do not, it is our children, every life on our planet, and the earth itself, that will suffer the consequences.

Humanity accepts the senseless deaths of innocents, their life ending before their appointed time, as a normal part of life.

Every needless death though harms all.

Their spirit, a piece of god present within each, will no longer be present to share its wisdom and unconditional love with the world.

No one life is, or ever has been better, more important, than another's.

Every life, regardless of our differences, accomplishments, or genus, each with a spirit, a piece of god within, is intimately connected to the other.

Each, therefore, deserves to be equally respected, selflessly helped in their time of need, and treated with unconditional love.

Our upbringing emphasizes achievement to define our purpose in life.

Money, material possessions, our prominence in the world, identify that success.

Though we may have achieved all our goals, without the acceptance of the loving spiritual path, selflessly sharing our spirit's wisdom and unconditional love to help others succeed in their life as well, our life will have been led without true meaning or purpose.

The world in which we live is insane, accepting greed, inequity, prejudice; war, starvation, homelessness, as a normal part of life.

Absolutely none of these things need occur.

We are meant to live in an enlightened world, where we selflessly help each other in our times of need.

Only by challenging our current beliefs may we end this insanity, allowing us all to live in a world of love rather than fear; the world we were always meant to live in.

How many more innocent children must be hungry, neglected, senselessly die, before genuine change ends their suffering?

They are too young to understand prejudice, inequity, greed, wondering why others do not believe their lives are worthwhile.

Only when humanity genuinely realizes every life, regardless of our differences, achievements, or genus, is equally valuable, will true change happen, allowing all to suffer no more and for each to discover our life's genuine purpose as well.

Humanity's diverse beliefs divide rather than unite us.

They are the underlying cause of war, prejudice, inequity, and most other man-made problems and injustices.

With the embrace of spirituality, realizing every life, each with a spirit, a piece of god within, is intimately connected and equally important, there is but one inherent belief defining all of humanity.

It is unconditional love, shared without conditions, to benefit all.

Our world is in agony, being destroyed by humanity's indifference and greed.

If change is not imminent, our planet will simply wait until humanity is no more, then restore its grandeur to the pristine world it once was before they irrevocably damaged its untouched essence.

Most believe those who are wealthy, famous, have a prestigious job, are powerful.

This power, however, is temporary, fleeting, often influenced by changing circumstances in life.

True everlasting power may only be found within, then it must be shared selflessly to help all others remember this as well.

The life of a homeless, unknown, poor, minority person is, and has always been, as important as someone who is wealthy, famous, and has a prestigious job.

An animal, tree, or any other form of life is, and has always been, as important as a human being.

Every life, regardless of our differences, achievements, or genus, has a spirit, a piece of god within, and is, and always has been, as important as another's.

We live in a world where many struggle every day to survive, lacking food, shelter, safety, while others have these things in abundance.

Accepting this paradigm is the cause of greed, inequity, prejudice; of war, hunger, homelessness.

Only when all our resources are equally shared, our belief in entitlement challenged, may these problems truly be addressed, mitigating the unnecessary hardships so many must endure throughout the world.

We live in a world where many decisions are dictated by the wealthy and powerful to benefit the few.

We therefore spend money on bombs and bullets to kill others, rather than food and shelter to aid the hungry and homeless.

Only with a paradigm shift, where the benefits of all are always considered before those of the privileged few, may we mitigate this injustice, and may humanity begin on the spiritual path through life they were always meant to follow.

Living in a loud, chaotic, self-centered world, many become fearful, untrusting, causing them to withdraw into a shell to defend themselves.

It is only when we expose our inner core, our protective shield may be lowered, allowing us to pursue our genuine purpose in life.

All harmful emotions and behaviors are learned, resulting from living in a self-centered world, accepting the many myths we are taught as we learn to conform to society's beliefs.

Though some of what we learn is necessary to survive in the world, most encourage behaviors injuring others.

To end inequity, prejudice, indifference to the struggles of others, we must expand our focus from being only concerned about ourselves and success in life, to include selflessly caring for the success and well-being of every person and life on our planet as well.

Many pretend not to see, blind to the struggles of others, ignoring the realities visibly presented to them every day.

Believing there is little they may do to improve the lives of others, they do nothing.

We must all open our eyes, see the world as it is, then selflessly help change it by sharing our excess and unconditional love, our spirit, to help all who are needlessly struggling.

Inventions and scientific knowledge have furthered humanity's dominance on our planet and understanding of the universe.

Its growth, however, has mostly been limited to the material world in which we live.

Without further spiritual growth as well, understanding our true purpose in life is to selflessly share our spirit's wisdom and unconditional love with others, though our lives may be easier, our destiny will remain uncertain.

We live in a world of greed, prejudice, inequity.

Concerned only for ourself and our own success and survival, we rationalize the many needless struggles others suffer.

This is the cause of many of the self-inflicted problems humanity faces.

To mitigate these challenges, we must embrace love over fear, recognizing the equal importance of every life.

Most manmade challenges may be ended today.

Technology exists to end hunger, homelessness, climate change.

Greed, prejudice, inequity, may also be mitigated with the acceptance of the unconditional loving spiritual path through life, equally respecting the needs of every life, regardless of our differences, rather than the desires of only our own.

Many seek happiness and purpose in the world, believing money, material possessions, family, will allow them to find them there.

Though they may believe, having achieved all their goals, they have discovered happiness and purpose, it is an illusion, propagated by the ego, our learned beliefs.

True happiness and purpose may not be found in a self-centered world.

They must first be discovered within, embracing the wisdom and unconditional loving messages of our spirit, then selflessly shared with others so they may find happiness and purpose in their life as well.

After a preventable tragedy arising from prejudice, starvation, violence, resulting from the greed and power of the few to impose their will on others, thoughts and prayers are no longer enough.

Every life, regardless of our differences, beliefs, or accomplishments, is equally important; its loss is incalculable.

Only when this is truly realized and accepted will thoughts and prayers for needless deaths no longer be necessary and the spiritual evolution of humanity finally become a reality.

~ *451* ~

The world is endlessly divided by race, ethnicity, religion, wealth, and in hundreds of other ways.

Every division, caused by humanity's need to justify their superiority to another, divides us, furthering its harmful beliefs and actions.

Prejudice, inequity, war, are but a few of the outcomes of living in such a divisive self-centered world.

To cure this affliction, humanity must recognize and respect the genuine value and equal importance of every life, regardless of our differences, then treat each as we ourselves wish others to treat us.

Every life, regardless of our differences or genus, is inextricably connected to each other, linked by a universal spirit, a piece of god present within each.

Though humanity is the dominant, most intelligent species on our planet, it has never been more important than any other form of life or each other.

It is only when this insight is truly understood that the spiritual evolution of our planet may finally begin.

The world is endlessly divided; race, religion, wealth, are but three of hundreds of ways we differentiate ourselves from each other.

We do this to convince ourselves we are better, more successful than others, validating our superiority to another.

Our divisions, however, are the cause of most manmade problems in the world.

Though we may look, believe, act differently, it is our similarities that truly define us.

No one life, regardless of our differences, is, or ever has been, more important than another's.

Only when this spiritual tenet is truly understood, may humanity's hardships be mitigated and the future of our planet assured.

What will humanity's legacy be when, due to its self-destructive tendencies, it destroys our planet and all who inhabit it?

Will we be remembered for kindness and empathy, or will we be remembered for our indifference, prejudice, and inability to help each other?

If we do not choose which path we will follow, our legacy may soon be chosen for us.

We live in a very polarized world; instead of seeing our similarities, all we perceive are our differences.

Humanity endlessly divides themselves, isolating us from each other.

Only by embracing our common bond, the universal spirit, a piece of god present within every life, rather than our differences, may many of humanity's self-inflicted challenges be mitigated and their future be assured.

There is never a reason to accept the absurdity of war, senselessly extinguishing the light of another.

These pointless deaths benefit and enrich the few, leading to the demise of so many.

Life is far too precious to allow such meaningless deaths.

It is time to reject the premise war is an inevitable part of life; it is not.

Instead, we must embrace the unlimited potential life presents, sincerely caring and helping each other, rather than thoughtlessly causing them harm for no discernible reason.

Every person, regardless of their circumstances in life, may change the world.

Wealth, power, fame, are not required to achieve this.

By fully embracing the spiritual path, then selflessly sharing the spirit's wisdom and unconditional loving beliefs with others, we may awaken in them a long dormant feeling, beginning them on a path to help change the world as well.

Humanity's differences are used to justify their feelings of superiority to others.

It is only when we see our similarities rather than our differences that our world may finally unite in peace, allowing our children to live in a world of love rather than fear.

Many view the world through a self-centered lens, concerned only for what is best for themselves, rather than for others.

If we do not commit to taking care of each other and our planet, though the earth may survive, humanity and all life on it, may no longer grace its soil.

The spiritual path always considers what is best for everyone, rather than only ourselves.

It involves selflessly sharing our spirit's wisdom and unconditional love with all others, to aid their journey through life.

If humanity does not willingly choose this path, the choice may soon be made for us.

The ego, our learned beliefs, helps us survive in the world; the spirit though, present to give our lives meaning by sharing its wisdom and unconditional love to help guide our life's choices, allows us to find purpose in our lives as well.

Most, accepting their acquired beliefs, look for meaning in the self-centered world; it may not be found there.

Meaning must first be found within, then must be selflessly shared to help others find meaning in their lives as well.

We each choose our destiny; it has little to do with wealth, fame, race, religion, or any other comparison differentiating us from each other.

If we choose to seek our destiny by following the self-centered beliefs of the world, then, though we may be successful in life, our destiny is to live a life of mediocrity, one without true purpose or meaning.

If, however, *despite* our circumstances in life, we follow the spiritual path instead, selflessly sharing our spirit's wisdom and unconditional love to help others, our destiny will be to live a life full of eternal love, inner peace, and an understanding of our life's true purpose.

Humanity believes they are not only superior to all other forms of life, but some believe their life, due to their differences, is more valuable than others as well.

Only when we recognize the genuine worth of every life, regardless of our appearance, accomplishments, or genus, is exactly the same, may our species evolve and our planet, and all who inhabit it, flourish.

By blindly accepting the self-centered beliefs we are taught, we are thrust into a chaotic world, destined, despite our success in life, to endlessly struggle seeking happiness, love, and meaning.

We awaken when we begin to question the truth of these beliefs.

We become enlightened when we understand true happiness, love, and meaning may not be found in a self-centered world.

They may only be discovered within, then by selflessly sharing our spirit's wisdom and unconditional love to help others find true happiness, love, and meaning in their lives, we will find these in abundance in our life as well.

Since humanity is the dominant species on our planet, they believe their lives are more important than other less evolved life forms.

There are some who even believe, due to our many differences, their life is more important than others.

When we awaken, beginning to sense the first quiet messages of our spirit within, we start to question these beliefs.

When we realize every life, regardless of our appearance or genus, each having a spirit, a piece of god within, is equally important, we begin on a journey to discover our true life's purpose.

Humanity believes, because of their intelligence, they are better, their lives more important than all other forms of life and the planet that sustains us all.

This self-centered view of the world is the cause of many of our self-inflicted problems.

Humanity is, and never has been, better than any other form of life or each other.

Only when we accept this premise, may our many challenges start to mitigate and our planet begin to heal.

Many close their eyes, pretending not to see the struggles of others, ignoring their pain, tears, hunger, senseless deaths.

We must all open our eyes, pretend no more, selflessly help all who are struggling.

Only then may their challenges be mitigated and our world finally begin to evolve.

Most define their value by their accomplishments in the world.

Money, job, material possessions, family, are but a few ways they determine their worth.

In truth, our value may not be found in a self-centered world.

To discover the genuine worth of a life, we must first look within, then selflessly share our wisdom and unconditional love, our spirit, with all others.

Many believe who they are is decided by their circumstances in life.

Race, ethnicity, religion, wealth, are but a few of the numerous ways we identify ourselves in a very divided world, further isolating, rather than uniting us with each other.

Though we all appear, act, believe differently, we are truly the same.

We are spirit, a piece of god present within each, intimately connecting us to each other.

Only when we put aside our insignificant superficial differences, embracing instead our similarities, may humanity evolve and our planet begin to heal.

Many believe they cannot change the struggles so many others endure.

This is a lie, fabricated by a self-centered world, to convince us to accept the status quo.

We must each challenge this illusion.

Only then may our world begin to evolve, as we start to recognize there is much we can all do together.

A majority of the world, accepting the self-centered status quo, allows life to impose its will on them.

It is time for us to impose our collective will on life instead by challenging this myth.

Only by confronting our learned beliefs and embracing the spiritual guidance within, may we begin to challenge society's norms, helping to bring genuine change to the world.

Living in a very divided world, separated by religion, ethnicity, wealth, race, and in hundreds of other ways, many become prejudiced, believing others different from them are not as deserving.

These differences are used to rationalize war, inequity, apathy.

We are all children of the world, related by a common purpose, intimately linked together by a spark of the divine, present within each.

Only by remembering it is our similarities, not our differences, that will ultimately define our life, may we begin to bring genuine change to an indifferent world.

We live in a world where self-preservation dictates our beliefs, thoughts, and actions, causing us to ignore the struggles of others.

To rediscover our humanity, we must reunite with our loving spirit within, then selflessly share its compassion, wisdom, and love to help others in need.

Humanity has become resigned, believing the numerous hardships so many suffer are an inevitable part of life.

They therefore immunize themselves, believing there is little they may do to bring meaningful change.

We must no longer allow apathy to define our life.

Instead, we each may help change the world by selflessly helping all who are struggling.

Only then may our world begin to evolve, allowing our children to grow up in a world of unconditional love, rather than to continue to live in a world of endless fear.

Regardless of our circumstances in life, we each may choose the path we will follow.

It matters not whether we are wealthy or poor, important or unknown; nor does it matter our race, ethnicity, sex, or any other differences between us.

If we choose to live our life in fear, believing the many challenges resulting from living in a self-centered world may not be changed, we will not know true love or find genuine meaning in our life.

If, however, we choose to follow the spiritual path instead, selflessly sharing our wisdom and unconditional love, our spirit with others, we will then discover a world of hope, eternal love, and endless possibilities.

Though humanity has made great technological advances, it is their lack of a moral, spiritual center that may lead to their demise.

Man-made problems, too numerous to list, causing hardships for many, dominate our self-centered world.

To break this cycle of despair, we must rediscover the wisdom and unconditional loving messages of our spirit within, then share our resources, excess, and love selflessly with all in need.

Laws are created by man, whose beliefs are often influenced by their self-centered upbringing.

This may result in discrimination and inequity based on religion, ethnicity, race, wealth, and in numerous other ways.

Any law hurting another in any way is immoral.

Regardless of the offense, all laws should always be predicated on not allowing harm to another.

When injury is caused, only by challenging the status quo may justice truly be served.

Many struggle every day, our mind and spirit battling within for dominance.

When the ego, our self-centered beliefs, dominates, our challenges that day control our life.

When our spirit, however, is predominant, we will know inner peace, true happiness, genuine love, and experience a feeling of purpose.

Before we are born our light is blinding.

With our birth, the ego, our learned beliefs, begins to dull our light.

The more we accept these beliefs, the darker our light becomes.

We then spend the rest of our life trying to find our lights brilliance once more.

Every life and the earth itself are part of a collective.

Each piece, regardless of genus, is equally important in the survival and continued existence of the other.

Only by realizing this essential spiritual tenet, treating each part of the collective with respect, empathy, and love, may the future for our planet and all who dwell on it, be ensured.

Author's Note:

It is my hope your understanding of awakening, enlightenment, and spirituality has been enhanced by reading book 3 of '*Our Search for Meaning*'. If it has, could you please take a few minutes to: "Write a Review" and recommend this book on social media and to your friends and family.

Our Search for Meaning was written to try to awaken and help others who are awakened more fully understand what enlightenment is, so their spiritual journey through life may be more fully realized.

Thank you for taking the time to read:

'*Our Search for Meaning*' – *Book 3.* Please consider reading the other two books in this series as well.

Books by Ken Luball

The four Spiritual books in *The Awakening Tetralogy*:
Today I Am Going to Die: Choices in Life
The Spirit Guide: Journey Through Life
Tranquility: A Village of Hope
The Illusion of Happiness: Choosing Love Over Fear

■■■

A Mystical Trilogy. '*Our Search for Meaning*' - a series of three books of thoughtful easily understandable spiritual reflections about awakening, enlightenment, spirituality, & the meaning of life.

****

A Spiritual Duology: '*Spiritual Reflections*' - Two books of spiritual reflections using metaphor, imagery, and spiritual insight to explore themes of awakening, enlightenment, and the human pursuit of meaning.

■■■

The first three stories in *The Awakening Tetralogy* are written in the first person, following the spiritual journey through life of a child, as they learn the lessons needed during their life to awaken and become enlightened. These books are written in an understandable, interesting, unique narrative, which is both thought-provoking and engaging.

To find links for each of these nine books please visit my website: kenluball.com.

About Ken

Peace, Love, & Light

■■

My name is Ken Luball ~ Spiritual ~ Seeker ~ Author ~
Guide ~
****

Ever since I was a young child, I knew my purpose in life; it was for me to awaken, find enlightenment, and share my experience and knowledge with others. To reach those lofty aspirations though, I first had to navigate through quite a few unexpected detours in my life. Though I was brought up in a religious family, it did not help me hear the messages from my spirit guide, Bodhi. If anything, religion only further isolated me, teaching me to accept the ego's view of religion rather than Bodhi's. It was not until after I stopped following a formal religion, I finally was able to embrace spirituality, and with this embrace, I awoke.

Spirituality is the belief there is a piece of god, a spirit, within everything that has life, and, because of this, all life is important, equal, and connected. After I awoke, no longer having the dogma of religion handicapping my views, I was suddenly free to explore this philosophy of life more deeply. Only then did I become aware of the mask I wore and the impenetrable wall I had erected around my heart; the mask and wall allowed me to survive in the world. I would always smile, appear happy, though I would often feel intense anxiety within. This was something I never really understood until the moment I confronted my ego. Little did I know these survival mechanisms would have a profound effect on me for the majority of my life. By protecting me from emotional pain, they also isolated me from my family, everyone else in my life, and even from myself. No one could hurt me because I did not allow anyone to get close enough to do so. In turn, no one could love me or was I able to truly love another either. This superficial life, one devoid of risk or pain, left me alone in a sea of people.

It took many years before the first cracks in my wall formed and before I could loosen the mask I constantly wore. It took me almost an entire lifetime to awaken and begin my journey toward enlightenment.

After I was clearly able to hear my spirit guide, Bodhi, I realized everything I had learned from my ego throughout my life was untrue. I had looked for love and happiness in the job I had, the money I made, things I owned, and through my wife and children. With the exception of the latter, I finally realized none of those things truly mattered. This does not mean I am ungrateful to my ego, however. It taught me coping skills and allowed me to succeed, or at least what I thought success was. Though my ego still remains with me, it has taken a more secondary role in my life now, relinquishing its former primary role to my spirit guide, Bodhi.

Decisions were now required. While it was tempting to take this newly found state of being, withdraw from society and all the hate, fear, cruelty, poverty, and greed that plagues it, I knew within myself, this knowledge was to be shared with others. That is my destiny. Therefore, I have written A 𝕸𝖞𝖘𝖙𝖎𝖈𝖆𝖑 𝕿𝖗𝖎𝖑𝖔𝖌𝖞: *'Our Search for Meaning'*: a series of three books of thoughtful easily understandable spiritual reflections about life; A 𝕾𝖕𝖎𝖗𝖎𝖙𝖚𝖆𝖑 𝕯𝖚𝖔𝖑𝖔𝖌𝖞: *'Spiritual Reflections'*: two books of spiritual reflections using metaphor, imagery, and spiritual insight to explore themes of awakening, enlightenment, and the human pursuit of meaning; and 𝕿𝖍𝖊 𝕬𝖜𝖆𝖐𝖊𝖓𝖎𝖓𝖌 𝕿𝖊𝖙𝖗𝖆𝖑𝖔𝖌𝖞: the first three stories in *The Awakening Tetralogy* follow the spiritual journey through life of a child, as they learn the lessons needed during their life to awaken and become enlightened. It is my hope you will read these books, and in doing so, begin a new adventure; one where you will awaken and further your journey toward enlightenment with your spirit within.

I do not know if these books will be widely read in my lifetime, though I hope one day they may help others awaken and find enlightenment as well.

"We are all on a spiritual journey of love & peace; together may we spread light throughout the world."

To read more of Ken's life-changing reflections visit his website: kenluball.com

www.ingramcontent.com/pod-product-compliance
Lightning Source LLC
Chambersburg PA
CBHW060401130626